The Religious Poetry
of
Vladimir Solovyov

Other Works of Vladimir Solovyov
Translated or Edited by Boris Jakim

The White Lily. 1995
Poems of Sophia. With Laury Magnus. 1996
At the Dawn of Mist-Shrouded Youth. With Laury Magnus. 1999
Lectures on Divine Humanity. 1995
The Crisis of Western Philosophy. 1996
The Concept of God. 1999
The Justification of the Good. 2005

THE
RELIGIOUS POETRY

OF

VLADIMIR SOLOVYOV

Selected, Edited, and Translated
by
BORIS JAKIM

SEMANTRON PRESS

First published in the USA
by Semantron Press
an imprint of Sophia Perennis 2008
Reprinted by Semantron Press
an imprint of Angelico Press 2014
© Boris Jakim 2014

For information, address:
Angelico Press, Ltd.
4709 Briar Knoll Dr. Kettering, OH 45429
www.angelicopress.com

Library of Congress Cataloguing-in-Publication Data

Solovyov, Vladimir Sergeyevich, 1853–1900
The religious poetry of Vladimir Solovyov / selected, edited,
and introduced by Boris Jakim; translated by Boris Jakim
and Laury Magnus.—1st ed.

p. cm.
ISBN 978 1 59731 279 0 (pbk: alk. paper)
1. Solovyov, Vladimir Sergeyevich, 1853–1900—Translations
into English. 2. Religious poetry, Russian. I. Jakim, Boris. II. Magnus Laury.
III. Bulgakov, Sergei Nikolaevich, 1871–1944. IV. Title.
PG3470.S7A6 2008
891.71'3—dc22   2008022585

Cover image: detail from *The Battle of Montmirail,*
by Emile-Jean-Horace Vernet, 1822
Cover design: Michael Schrauzer

CONTENTS

Editor's Introduction

1.

VLADIMIR SOLOVYOV had a profound relationship, mystical and personal, with Sophia—a relationship which finds its most complete expression in his poetry. In his most autobiographically revealing and most mystically saturated poem, "Three Meetings," Solovyov describes his intensest encounter with Sophia:

> The fragrance of roses wafted from earth and heaven.
> And in the purple of the heavenly glow
> You gazed with eyes full of an azure fire.
> And your gaze was like the first shining
> Of universal and creative day.
>
> What is, what was, and what will be were here
> Embraced within that one fixed gaze… The seas
> And rivers all turned blue beneath me, as did
> The distant forest and the snow-capped mountain heights.
>
> I saw it all, and all of it was one,
> One image there of beauty feminine…
> The immeasurable was confined within that image.
> Before me, in me, you alone were there.
>
> O radiant one! I'm not deceived by you.
> I saw all of you there in the desert…
> In my soul those roses shall not fade
> Wherever it is that life's billows may rush me.[*]

---

[*] See p. 105 of the present volume.

2.

Vladimir Solovyov (1853–1900) was one of the most remarkable figures of the 19th century. He was the most important Russian speculative thinker of that century, publishing major works on theoretical philosophy, the philosophy of religion, and ethics. He also produced sensitive literary criticism and incisive essays on current political, social, and ecclesiastical questions.

He was the son of a famous father—the eminent historian Sergei Solovyov, who wrote one of the great histories of Russia. Steeped in an atmosphere of intense intellectuality, Vladimir was an extraordinarily precocious, devout, and sensitive child. At the age of seven, he had become so impassioned a reader of the *Lives of the Saints* that his parents, themselves zealous, had to restrain his ardor. The family's life was harmonious, but its atmosphere was one of severe piety, and the future philosopher long remained immersed in the dreams of early childhood. "A strange child was I/And strange dreams did I see" (see poem 9 below), Solovyov later wrote about himself. These "strange dreams" never lost their power over his soul, and in some sense the realm of mystical dreams always remained his spiritual home.

Between the ages of fourteen and eighteen, Solovyov lost his childhood faith and was possessed by a passionate and violent atheism; he "passed through all the phases of theoretical negation," as he himself put it. But the return to faith also began in his adolescent years—through exposure to Spinoza, from whom Solovyov took not only the vital sense of God's reality but also a vivid experience of the spiritual all-unity of the world. Indeed, this return to religion grew into the full-fledged vocation of a religious philosopher. He published one important work after another in his twenties: *The Crisis of Western Philosophy: Against the Positivists* (1874), *The Philosophical Principles of Integral Knowledge* (1877), *A Critique of Abstract Principles* (1877–1880), and *Lectures on Divine Humanity* (1877–1881).

By the early 1880s Solovyov had turned to a new project: the reunification of the churches. He was the first contemporary thinker to devote himself to this task, and he has been called "perhaps the most important proponent of ecumenical principles in Europe after Leibniz."[†] He linked the reunification of the churches with his utopian project of a "future theocracy," the establishment of an ideal Christian society harmoniously headed by an emperor and a hierarch, both divinely empowered.

Solovyov's last decade was marked by disillusionment with his theocratic project, a withdrawal from ecclesiastical politics, and a return to theoretical philosophy. During this decade he wrote a highly original book on love, *The Meaning of Love* (1897), and a treatise on ethics and social philosophy, *The Justification of the Good* (1892–94). In the last years of his life, obsessed by a gathering sense of the palpable power of evil in the world, he wrote his final work, *Three Conversations Concerning War, Progress, and the End of History, Including a Short Tale of the Antichrist* (1900). This extraordinary work, focusing on the impending apocalypse and the temporary reign of cosmic evil symbolized in the figure of the Antichrist, casts a prophetically pessimistic look forward at the 20th century.

As George L. Kline points out, the eminent theologian Hans Urs van Balthasar

> sees in Solovyov the "greatest artist of [conceptual] order and organization"—after St. Thomas—in the entire history of thought, a thinker who borrows from all systems after purging them of their "negations." His philosophical and religious thought is a "work of art" on a large scale—a drama, an epic, and a hymn to the universe.[*]

3.

In the *Lectures on Divine Humanity*, Solovyov outlines a doctrine of Sophia, the wisdom of God, which is so important in the further development of Russian religious thought. But for him, Sophia is more than a theory, more than a metaphysical construct; she is also a feminine being. He appears to have had three visions of this personified Wisdom, the fair

† See George L. Kline, "Russian Religious Thought" in *Nineteenth Century Religious Thought in the West*, ed. Ninian Smart et al., Cambridge University Press, vol. 2, 1985, p. 213.

* Ibid, p. 217.

lady Sophia, visions which he recorded in his poem "Three Meetings."*
He first saw her when he was a boy of nine, while attending the liturgy in
a church in Moscow (the vision was the resolution of a curious "love
affair"). In 1875 (at the age of twenty-two) he saw her again while pursu-
ing research at the British Museum. He heard a voice telling him to go to
Egypt, which he proceeded to do. There, awakening from sleep in the
desert, he had his third vision of Sophia (see the poetic description of this
encounter in the first section of the Editor's Introduction).

The *Lectures on Divine Humanity* introduce and briefly develop a
philosophical theory of Sophia. Solovyov identifies Sophia with the
world soul considered as the active principle, a principle which progres-
sively exemplifies in the created world the eternal all-uniting idea in the
Logos.† Sophia is also identified with the end of this process, with that
which is produced, i.e., with spiritualized humanity, the community of
persons united in Divine Humanity. Sophia is conceived in a variety of
ways: as the eternal ideal prototype of humanity, as the world soul
actively engaged in actualizing this prototypical idea, and as the fully
developed divine-human organism. She is portrayed both as the active
principle of the creative process and as its realized goal, the kingdom of
God, the society of those participating in Divine Humanity.‡

Solovyov is the founder of the sophiological current in modern Rus-
sian philosophy. His sophiology was further developed and often trans-
mogrified in the work of the philosophers E. N. Trubetskoi (1863–1920),
Pavel Florensky (1882–1937), and Sergius Bulgakov (1871–1944).
Solovyov's visions of Sophia were also a source of inspiration for Rus-
sian symbolist poets such as Alexander Blok (1880–1921) and Andrei
Belyi (1880–1934).

* See pp. 99–107 of the present volume.

† See Frederick C. Copleston, *Russian Religious Philosophy. Selected Aspects*, Search
Press, Kent, England, 1988, p. 84.

‡ The notion of Divine Humanity is rooted in the Creed of Chalcedon, which
defines the dual nature of Christ, divine and human, and expresses the process whereby
man cooperates with God, leading to the transfiguration of humanity and fusing the
entire human community into a heavenly Church without barriers between denomina-
tions. This process has its central focus in the Incarnation of God in Jesus.

Solovyov's poetry, little known outside of Russia, is a necessary comple-
ment to his philosophy. In his poetry, he often sketches out ideas that he
later fully develops in the philosophy. His poetry might be seen as evolv-
ing from an ascetic opposition between heaven and earth in the early
poems, through a period when he saw light shining forth from the dark-
ness of matter, to a later period of synthesis of the heavenly and earthly.
Of particular importance are the love poems addressed to various
women (especially the "love of his life," Sophia [!] Khitrovo). Solovyov
often wrote that earthly love has its highest meaning as a form of mani-
festation of the World Soul, of the Eternal Feminine. He brought a mys-
tical meaning into his relations with women, which often imparted to his
feelings a religiously ecstatic character. He considered love a means to
escaping the ego, a means to allowing human beings to live not in them-
selves but in other human beings, thus creating the conditions for a
future universal-human unity.

Of particular note are what can be called Solovyov's "Poems of
Sophia," the short poems nos. 7–9 in the present volume and the long
poem "Three Meetings." These poems address the most important expe-
rience of Solovyov's life: his vision of Sophia (he sometimes refers to her
as "goddess" or "empress") in the Egyptian desert at the end of Novem-
ber 1875. The three short poems were written soon after the event
occurred, whereas the elaborate "Three Meetings" was written almost
twenty-three years after the experience in the desert.

The first of the short poems, "All in azure did my empress," is a mere
notation of the fact of Sophia's appearance to Solovyov. The second
poem, "My empress has a lofty palace," describes how Solovyov has
fallen from the original vision in the desert, but how Sophia had not
abandoned him. We see in the third poem, "Near, far off, not here, not
there," that he is no longer tempted to wander spiritually. He has found
his true "homeland," far from the "midnight land . . . of freezing mists
and blizzards." He has found his true homeland in Sophia's "greeting,"
in her "magic speech."

He waited until 26–29 September 1898 to compose the celebrated
"Three Meetings." It could well be that the most powerful impetus for
his writing this poem in 1898 was his sense that death was near (he died
in 1900), and that he had to leave posterity a record of his personal

encounters with Sophia. If the three much earlier poems are "snapshots" of the vision in the desert and of the effects that it produced in his soul, "Three Meetings" presents this vision panoramically, as it were.

"Three Meetings" is a study in azure, in the heavenly. One of the things we know with certainty about Sophia is that she comes clothed in sky-blue, that she is formed out of heavenly elements. This azure radiance fills both the church and Solovyov's soul—indeed it fills the whole universe: "Azure was all around; azure was in my soul." Years later, at the British Museum, he felt that "all around was filled with golden azure / And before me she was shining again." And in the desert in Egypt, he saw her "with eyes full of an azure fire." The universe became blue: "the seas / And rivers all turned blue beneath me, as did / The distant forest and the snow-capped mountain heights."

Standing somewhat apart from the poems of Sophia but nevertheless allied with them is the sophianic comedy, "The White Lily." This play is perhaps the greatest example of the comical-mystical genre, a genre probably invented by Solovyov. Deep mystical longings and ecstatic outpourings coexist with pratfalls, guffaws, and buffoonery. St. John the Divine coexists with the Marx Brothers, Boehme with the Three Stooges. The approach to the Holy of Holies is accompanied by laughter, sometimes of a very crude kind. But there is no laughter in the sanctuary itself: buffoonery and holiness do not merge consubstantially in Solovyov. (By the way, we find a similar buffoonery—and a similar awe before the Divine—in "Three Meetings.")

"The White Lily," which Solovyov called a "mystery-jest," is autobiographical in character: Solovyov's alter-ego, the noble and melancholy Chevalier de Mortemir, yearns for Sophia (embodied in White Lily), and, accompanied by his comic companions, led by the ridiculous guide (a foreshadowing of Groucho Marx and W. C. Fields), Don't-Spit-On-The-Table, he travels to "a large neglected garden near southern Tibet" to seek her. There, Mortemir meets the beloved "bear of [his] soul," who dies and out of whom the White Lily is released like a butterfly out of a cocoon. "They embrace and, rising into the air, suddenly go over into the fourth dimension. White lilies and red roses grow on the former grave of the bear."* And so, Mortemir has had his final meeting

* See p. 148 of the present volume.

with Sophia and he has gone with her, through death, to the "fourth dimension," a jocular name for the paradise where man once had (and someday will once again have) a permanent clear vision of Sophia.

There is much joking in "The White Lily," but when all is said and done, Solovyov did not joke about Sophia: twenty-three years after the original vision, as described in "Three Meetings," she remains his "eternal beloved." For all these years he remained in love with the sky, with the heavenly Sophia (the youthful spring) who bends over the dark earth (the somber winter). He did not live in the same world the rest of us are forced to live in: "defeated by . . . [Sophia's] . . . mysterious beauty / The ocean of humdrum life receded far away."* As we see, in his poetry, Solovyov was able to penetrate beneath the crust of rough matter and see the incorruptible royal purple of divinity. The vision became his permanent state.

5.

The present selection of Solovyov's poetry contains all the short lyric verse, most of which is translated here into English for the first time. Poems 7–9 and "Three Meetings" appeared previously in Vladimir Solovyov's *Poems of Sophia* (Variable Press, 1996). *The White Lily*, revised by Boris Jakim and Laury Magnus for this edition, previously appeared in a translation by Boris Jakim published by The Variable Press. The present edition of the "mystical and lyrical" verse also includes the political poetry, which is closely linked to Solovyov's theocratic conceptions. The comic verse is omitted except for the "Parodies of the Symbolists." Of the three plays, only the sophianic "White Lily" is included.

The translations are mainly done in iambics, with no attempt made to imitate Solovyov's rhymes. The translators felt it more important to reproduce the spiritual sense of the poems than the external form. They did attempt, however, to make the verse "sound" like poetry, not like prose. The poems are arranged and enumerated in chronological order

---

* See p. 106 of the present volume.

[7]

according to the most authoritative Russian edition: *Vladimir Solovyov: Stikhotvoreniya i shutochnye p'esy* (Vladimir Solovyov: Poems and Comic Plays), edited and annotated with an introduction by Z. G. Mintz, published by Sovetsky Pisatel', Biblioteka Poeta osnovana M.Gor'kim, Large Series, 2nd edition, Leningrad, 1974.

⊕

The appendix contains an important essay on Solovyov's poetry by the eminent Russian Orthodox theologian Sergius Bulgakov. Bulgakov attempts to indicate the relationship between Solovyov's poetry and his philosophy, and to affirm the mystical roots of Solovyov's work as a whole. The editor agrees with Bulgakov's assessment of Solovyov as a poet but not with his assessment of Solovyov as a philosopher.

Short Poems

1.

Nature does not permit us
To lift the veil of her beauty.
And you'll never extract by machine
What your spirit can't divine in her.
(1872)

2.

To Prometheus*

When your soul sees in one light
Falsehood with truth, evil with good,
And embraces the world entire
In one salutation of love,
What is and what is past;

When you learn the bliss of reconciliation;
When your mind comprehends
That only in the phantom of infantile opinion
Do falsehood and evil live—

Then will the hour come—the last hour of creation...
And with one ray your light will dissipate
A whole world of mist-shrouded vision
In the heavy dream of earth:

The barriers are falling; the fetters are melted
By divine fire,
And eternal morning rises to new life
In all creatures, and all is in the One.
(August 1874)

* This poem reflects the young Solovyov's infatuation with Nietzsche. The myth of Prometheus is seen as foretelling that, one day, heaven will merge with earth. — ED.

3.

Only a year ago in an agony of pain,
In insane agony I parted from you,
And it seemed that, together with you,
I had lost life, light, and happiness forever.

Only a year has passed and you have vanished
Into the nothingness of forgetting, like
An ancient, ancient dream, and only at times do I
remember for an instant
The former days wherein I dreamed that dream.
(23 December 1874)

4.

Just as in the pure azure of a sea grown still
The entire glory of the heavens is reflected,
So does eternal goodness appear to us
In the light from a free spirit's passion.

But the deep that in its powerful expanse lies motionless
Is that same deep that is in turbulent agitation:
The spirit that is powerful and clear in free repose
Is the same spirit as in passionate desire.

Freedom and bondage, repose and agitation
Pass and reappear. But the spirit remains
Unchanged; and only in elemental striving
Can its power be revealed.
(March 1875)

5.

Within the dream of earth we are but shadows, shadows.
Life is a play of shadows,
A series of far-off reflections
Of days eternally luminous.

But the shadows merge already
And the former features
Of former vivid dreams
You will no longer recognize.

A gray, predawn darkness
Has clothed the whole of earth;
A welcome trepidation has
Seized hold of the prophetic heart.

Nor will the voice of prophecy deceive.
Believe, the shadow is passing.
Do not grieve: a new eternal day
Will soon be dawning.
(9 June 1875)

6.

Although we are forever chained—*
With chains invisible—to unearthly shores,
Yet must we follow in those chains
The circle that the gods have drawn for us.

---

* Written at the time of Solovyov's visit to London, where he was doing research at the British Museum (and had his second encounter with Sophia). This is the first of Solovyov's poems to clearly express his philosophical credo such as it was in the 1870's. See also the sophianic poems (numbers 7, 8, 9) and poem no. 11.—ED.

All that accepts the higher will
Does with its will another will
And under the impassive mask of matter
The divine fire everywhere is burning.
(between 29 June and 28 October 1875)

7.

All in azure did my empress[*]
Appear today before me.
My heart beat in sweet rapture
And my soul began to shine
With quiet light in rays of the dawning day.
But in the distance, burning low,
The cruel flame of the earthly fire still glowed.
(End of November 1875. Cairo)

8.

My empress has a lofty palace
With seven golden pillars.
My empress has a seven-pointed crown,
Inlaid with countless precious stones.

In my empress's green garden
Fair roses and lilies bloom,
And a silvery stream catches the reflection
Of curls and brow in its transparent waters.

But my empress does not hear what the stream whispers.
She does not so much as glance at the flowers:

* Poems 7, 8, and 9 pertain to Soloyvov's vision of Sophia in the Egyptian desert
(later elaborated in great detail in his poem "The Three Meetings'; see below). See the
introduction for a discussion of this key experience. — ED.

Sorrow beclouds the light of her azure eyes,
And all her reverie is full of grief.
She sees: far off in a midnight land
Amidst the freezing mists and blizzards,
Her beloved, whom she has forsaken, is perishing
In solitary combat with dark and evil powers.

She casts aside her diamond crown,
Abandons the golden palace, and, arriving,
An unexpected guest, at her faithless beloved's door,
She knocks upon it, her hand full of grace.

And bathed in light, she bends down over him
Like youthful springtime over somber winter
And, full of quiet tenderness,
Covers him with her radiant veil.

And the dark powers are stricken to the ground.
His whole being burns with a pure flame,
And with eternal love in her azure eyes
She softly speaks to her beloved: "I know

Your resolve is more inconstant than sea waves:
You vowed to keep fidelity to me. You have
Betrayed your vow—but could your betrayal
Really have caused my heart to change?"
(between the end of November 1875 and 6 March 1876, Cairo)

9.

Near, far off, not here, not there,
In realms of mystic reveries,
In a world invisible to mortal eyes,
In a world without laughter and without tears,

There it was, Goddess, that I first
Recognized you one misty night.
A strange child was I,
And strange dreams did I see.

It was in an alien guise that you appeared
To me. Your voice sounded obscure.
And as the obscure creation of a childish dream
I long regarded you.

Now you appear to me once more
With a caress of unexpected love.
I see you now not in a dream,
Your speech is clear to me.

I, who had been deafened in an alien world
By the roar of incoherent speech,
Suddenly heard within your salutation
The word of my homeland.

The voice of my homeland in your magic speech,
In the light of your azure eyes,
My homeland's reflection in ethereal rays.
In the golden color of your wondrous curls.

Everything by which my heart and my mind live,
Everything trembling here within my breast,
All powers of feeling, will, and thought
That are mine I've given into your hands.

That morose despot, the cold ego,
Sensing its death approaching, trembles.
The moment it sees you approaching from afar
It grows silent, pallid, and then flees.

Let it perish, arrogant fugitive!
In free bondage and in living death

I am the altar, and I am also the sacrifice and priest.
Tormented by bliss, I stand before you.
(Between the end of November 1875 and 6 March 1876. Cairo)

10.
Song of the Ophites*

A white lily with a rose,
With a red rose, we marry.
By mysterious dream prophetic
We find eternal truth.

Say the prophetic word!
Quickly cast your pearl into the cup!
Bind our dove
With new coils of the ancient serpent.

The free heart does not ache.
Should the pure dove fear the Promethean fire?
She feels her freedom
Within the mighty serpent's flaming rings.

Sing then of violent tempests.
In violent tempests we find peace...
A white lily with a rose,
With a red rose, we marry.
(Beginning of May 1876)

* This poem appears at the conclusion of "The White Lily" (see below). The Ophi-
tes (from the Greek: *ophis*, snake) were ancient gnostic sects who worshipped the snake
as a symbol of the dying and resurrected world soul. The white lily and the rose, as well
as the dove and the serpent, are mystical figures standing for the synthesis of the spiritual
and sensual principles.—ED.

11.

Vis Ejus integra si versa fuerit in terram[*]

He truly is beloved of the gods who in the spring
Of life has not crowned his head with myrtle,
Who only in reveries has been beckoned
By Cytherea's, golden empress's, gentle hand.
Not rich in gifts of the muses or the graces,
Let him hide the seed of ancient Chronos deep within
His heart and nourish it with somber thought.

Soon or late the flame, concealed, will break out.
It will flash out like lightning and embrace the earth in a broad fire.
And all that had been buried in the breast,
That sought in vain an image for itself:
The proud spirit's impulses and limitless tenderness of love,
All this will merge into a single power inexorable,
Embrace all human thoughts in a potent, magic stream,
Will close the golden chain and unite heaven with earth.
(16 May 1876)

12.

Whatever fate ordains I can't
Avert by my own powerless, childish will.
Abandoned and alone, I wander in a strange land,[†]
Longing for the skies of my homeland.

Far off in the distance shines my solitary star.
Her rays are beckoning me to a land that's magical.

---

[*] "Power will remain whole if it turns into earth"—a rather imprecise quotation from the mystical work "Tabula smaragdina," which Solovyov had encountered during his research at the British Museum in 1876. Cytherea is Aphrodite. In this poem, the return of the "golden age" is associated with the figure of Chronos.—ED.

[†] This poem was begun during Solovyov's stay in London, and is addressed to E. V. Romanova, his cousin, with whom he was in love when he was a very young man.—ED.

But inaccessible is that far land;
The ways that lead there promise me no joy.

Forgive me—and allow me one last wish,
One last sigh of my sick soul:
O, if for all the bitter suffering
That's been ordained for me by the will of fate

I could give you some golden days and years,
I could give you all the best of flowers,
So that in a new world of light and freedom
You could find rest from all life's cruelty!

So that the heavy visions of troubled dreams
Might scatter in the sunshine's rays,
So that, at the universal festival of rebirth,
You could arrive more pure and radiant than all.
(June 1875–1877)

13.

Look how transparent and pale are heaven's expanses,
How rays of light stretch across the half-bare garden...
"O, what a wonderful hour it is between
The darkness and the light."* What a holy silence!

Listen, look closely... silence and lethargy!
Does it not seem to you that the world will no longer awaken,
That the sun will never ascend out of the clouds,
That the last day has come?
(18 August 1878)

* Imprecise quotation from a poem of A.K. Tolstoy.—ED.

14.

Shapelier and more beautiful*
Than the gazelle of the savannah are you.
Your speech is infinite and fathomless.
Eve of Turan, Madonna of the steppes,
Be thou our intercessor before Allah.

Let all who have a heart that beats
Lie down before you, not rising from the dust.
Be thou our intercessor before Allah,
Madonna of the steppes, Eve of Turan!
(August 1878)

15.

Fragment†

What need have you of love or of caresses
If your own fire burns within your breast
And a whole fairy-tale world of magic
Converses so distinctly with your soul;
When in the bluing mist the path
Of everyday existence lies before you
But the goal has been reached beforehand
And victory has anticipated the battle;
When from your heart the silvery threads stretch forth
Into the realm of reverie...
O, gods eternal! Take the bitterness
Of my experience and return to me
The power of the first storms of spring!
(1878)

---

* This is the first poem dedicated to Sophia Khitrovo, with whom Solovyov was long
and tragically in love. "Eve of Turan" is what the French critic Vogüé called her: Turan
is the ancient Iranian name for Central Asia, land of Allah and of the Steppes. — ED.

† This poem was inspired by E. P. Polivanova, with whom Solovyov was once in
love. Part of this poem appeared later in "The White Lily" (see below). — ED.

16.

In former years, adversities of love
United us.
But passion's flame is not within our power
And my flame has gone out.

Let it be so that in the desert of the world
The two of us have been drawn together again—
We will now not reinfect each other with
The malady of love.

Spring has rushed past; all that remains to us
Is springtime's memory within the turbulence
Of life: just like a momentary dream,
Like being happy in a dream.
(1878)

17.

You are departing, and at the hour of separation[*]
My heart's no longer full of desire and prayer.
Worn out by long years of torment, needless falsehood, despair,
Ennui, it has surrendered and grown silent before fate.

Just as amid the sands of the arid steppe
There is a white row of abandoned graves,
So in my memory the tombs of the bright dreams
Of all my fruitless love, of feelings unexpressed
And words unuttered will find a cold peace there.

And if one day your beckoning voice
Sounds unexpectedly above these graves,

---

[*] Addressed by Solovyov to his beloved, Sophia Khitrovo.—ED.

Then only a stony echo from the desert
That lies between us two will send you,
In hardened waves, a cold and mute response.
(1880)

18.

Dedication to an Unpublished Comedy[*]

Do not expect harmonious, beautiful songs.
And do not ask dark autumn to bear flowers!
I have not known clear and radiant days,
And how many voiceless phantoms, motionless,
Have been abandoned on the darkling path.

This is the law: what's best is shrouded in mist,
Whereas what's near is either full of pain or comical.
We cannot escape this double extremity:
The harmony of the universe is created
Both out of ringing laughter and mute sobbing.

Let laughter resound like a free wave;
Our days are not worth indignation.
Poor muse, above the dim path but appear
Just once to us with a youthful smile
And, if but for a moment, mollify
The cruelty of life with a smile that is not cruel.
(1880)

19.

O, how much of pure azure there is
In you, how much of black, black clouds!
How clearly God's reflection shines above you,

* "The White Lily" (see below). — ED.

How full of torment burns the evil fire within you!
Within your soul the two eternal powers
Mysteriously collide with enmity invisible,
And, pressing close upon you, shadows of the two worlds,
Like an unruly mob, have grown strangely intertwined.

But I believe: the divine word,
With scintillating lightning, will pierce through this darkness,
And the black cloud will burst
Into the waste vale in powerful streams,

Will wash the vale with brightness of the dew,
Will sate the fire of the warring elements,
And the radiance of heaven's vault will be revealed
And motionlessly light all the earth's beauty.
(1881)

20.

It was in a land of fiercest blizzards,
Amid gray mists, that you appeared in the world,
And, poor child, caught between two hostile camps,
There was no place of refuge for you.

But not by militant cries,
By the ringing of armor or clash of swords will you
Be shaken; you stand pensively listening to
The mighty testament of days gone by:

How of old the supreme God had promised to
Reveal Himself to the Jews, his chosen,
And how the prophet, on fire with prayer,
Awaited his God there in the wilderness.

The subterranean rumbling and the great noise have passed,
The light of the sun is fading, and the earth has shuddered,

[21]

And fear has embraced the prophet, but
There is no God in fear.

Then came a noisy whirlwind, a violent breath
And a rumbling in the heights,
And a great fire, like a flash of lightning,
But there is no God in fire.

Everything has grown silent; the agitation is tamed.
The prophet did not wait in vain:
"A thin coldness bloweth"*—and in that
Mysterious breath he has divined his God.
(1882)

21.
Three Deeds

When to the sculptor the obedient stone
Presents itself in all its clearest beauty
And inspiration's powerful flame gives
Both life and flesh to your dream,
At that forbidden limit
Do not think that the deed has been completed,
And, Pygmalion, expect no love from the divine body!
Love needs fresh victory: the cliff
Hangs over the abyss,
Andromeda in agitation calls
You, Perseus, you, Alcides!†
The winged horse springs into the chasm,
The mirror shield is raised and overturned—
The dragon that has seen itself
Has plunged into the abyss.
Yet will the invisible enemy rise up.

---

* The last four stanzas are a paraphrase of 1 Kings 19:11–12. "A thin coldness blow-
eth" is the Slavonic Bible's rendition of what the King James version renders as "a still
small voice."—ED.

† Another name for Hercules.

Do not blow the horn of victory—
Soon, soon, the festival of happiness and
Of love will turn into a funeral feast.
The joyous cries will fade,
Sorrow and darkness and tears will appear again...
Eurydice, Eurydice,
Your love brought no salvation. But take heart!
Do not, with ailing soul, bow before fate,
Defenseless, weaponless,
But rather challenge death to fight you
To the death! And on the gloomy
Threshold, 'midst a crowd of weeping shades,
The enchanted gods will recognize you, Orpheus!
The waves of the all-triumphant song
Have shaken the vault of Hades, and
The lord of pallid death
Relinquishes Eurydice.
(1882)

22.

Having forgotten visions of a former time
Under a burning blizzard's alien power,
I once again heard the fading call
Of my mysterious beloved.

And with a cry of horror and of pain,
My spirit—an eagle caught up in an iron grip—
Quivered in its captivity,
Broke through the net and escaped into the heights.

And high above the clouds,
Before a sea of flaming miracles,
In an all-radiant holiness,
My spirit caught fire and disappeared.
(1882)

23.

A wingless spirit, earth-enslaved, a god
Who has forgotten himself and so has been forgotten...
It was but a mere dream, and winged again,
You hasten upward away from earthly cares.

An indistinct ray of a familiar shining,
The barely audible echo of an unearthly song,
And the former world once again rises before
Your sensitive soul in an unfading radiance.

It was only a dream, and in painful wakening
With an excruciating anguish will you await
Again a reflection of the unearthly vision,
Again an echo of the holy harmony.
(June 1883)

24.

In morning mist I went with wavering steps
Toward a mysterious and marvelous shore.
The dawn warred with the last remaining stars.
Dreams were still hovering, and, caught in dreams,
My soul sent forth its prayer to unknown gods.

On a cold white day I'm traveling as before,
On a solitary road in an unknown land.
The mist has lifted, the eye sees clearly
How arduous is the mountain path, and how far away,
How far away is everything I've dreamed of.

Until midnight I will keep on walking
With bold steps toward the wished-for shores,

Where, on the mountain, under new-made stars,
And all afire with triumphal lights,
My cherished temple lies awaiting me.
(1884)

25.

For A.A. Fet[^*] [19 October 1884]

Having flown over on swans' wings
The dual bound of space and of the aeons,
You overheard on the imperial heights
The living song of singers fallen silent.
And your sweet-sounding genius
Lured foreign gods unto our shores.
And beneath the ray of the resurrected songs
The northern snows have melted.

And to your song a splendid laurel
Blossomed upon the solitary steppe, resounding.
And the very eagle of native poetry
Flew down to you from heights the eye can't pierce.

26.

The fever of lonely impulses will not cure us of,
Yearning reverie will not save us from
Passions' fires, cruel and impure,
Wicked thoughts and lying vanity.

Neither in the deadly wilderness of humdrum life,
Nor at crossroads of idle thoughts and words

---

* The celebrated poet Afanasy Fet (1820–1892) was a close friend of Solovyov's. This poem refers to Fet's translations of classical poetry. — ED.

Can we retrieve the way to the lost holiness,
The trace of vanished gods.
No need of them! For in His infinite goodness
Our God did not abandon this His earth,
But He revealed to all a single path
From basest pride to humble eminence.

And Sion does not shake, nor does
The beauty of Sharon's sumptuous roses fade.
Above the living water, in a vale mysterious,
The sacred lily is incorruptible and pure.
(23 December 1884)

27.

L'onda dal mar divisa[*]

Once separated from the sea
The wave can know no peace.
It seethes like a hot spring
Or rolls on like a river.
It grumbles and it sighs
In freedom and in chains,
Yearning for the shoreless
And fathomless blue sea.
(1884)

* "The wave separated from the sea" (Italian). At the time of the writing of this poem, Solovyov was learning Italian, which was associated with his interest in the early Renaissance. — ED.

28.

*Dedicated to V.L. Velichko**

The season of spring's tempests has not passed,
And yet the winter has arrived already,
And, without warning, premature old age
Has told you life has dealt you a defeat.
And over chasms of aimless wandering,
A gray mist hangs suspended.
The soul feels nothing of past suffering,
Does not remember its old wounds.
And joyously inhaling mountain air,
I'm ready to set out on the new path
That far from flowers of faded May will take me,
And far from the hot summer's reveries.
(Beginning of January 1885)

29.

Supplanting the soul's raptures with deception's calculus,†
And living language of the gods with speech of slaves,
The muses' holy treasure with a noisy farce,
He managed to deceive the fools.

But when, crushed and disillusioned, he
Recalled the holy beauty in his anguish,
His mind, then impotent and chained to the dust of the earth,
Summoned in vain the incorruptible dream.

* Vasily L'vovich Velichko (1860–1903), a close friend of Solovyov's, later wrote the book: *Vladimir Solovyov: Life and Works* (1902).—ED.

† This poem represents a harsh critique of the aesthetics of the popular social poet Nikolai Nekrasov.—ED.

In vain was his desire to put the enthralling sounds
Of past love into his sorrowing verses.
He could not raise his unfeeling hands
And the pale phantom flew quietly away.
(January 1885)

30.

There, beneath the lime tree, at the railing,
A rendezvous has been appointed me.
And I go to keep it just like the meek lamb
That goes forth to the slaughter.

Everything is as it was before: on high
The ancient stars are twinkling,
And in the bushes nightingales
Are playing a concert with their ancient notes.

I'll not destroy the order of things...
But have compassion!
Do not torment my soul.
Release it to repentance.
(1886)

31.
Into the Promised Land
*Dedicated to A. P. Salomon**

"Abandon all at once your native land,
Your whole race, and your fathers' home,†
And, as the archer's arrows are obedient
To the archer, so be obedient to my words.

---

* Salomon (1853–1908), a journalist, was a friend of Solovyov's. — ED.
† God's command to Abraham (see Genesis 12:1). — ED.

[28]

Go forward without yearning for the past,
Go forward having forgotten it entirely.
Go forward—till I indicate to you
Just whither leads the summons of my love."

He rose from where he lay and, in tremulous perplexity,
Could not decide if this was truth or dream;
And all at once an unearthly breath came rushing
Above his head, and he could hear these words:

"From native Chaldean plains of many waters,
From mountain meadows of the Aramaic land,
From Harran, where you've lived till hoary age,
And from Ur, where your youthful years were passed—

Not for just one year,
Nor yet for many years,
But for all of eternity depart."

And so he gathered up a group of men.
And following the path of resurrected rays,
He set out into the distance, misty-blue,
Answering the mighty call of the mysterious speeches:

"The warm sea air blows straight into one's face.
Forward against the wind go forth.
And when the heavenly dome far off before you
Unfurls a vast expanse of the great waters,
Turn to the left and hasten forward
On a straight path. Rest on that path,
And toward midday look at the sun—
A city or a village will appear to one side,
But you must pass it by, and keep on going,
Keep on going, until I tell you this: Here!
I am with you forever.
Guard this my testament: with a pure heart
And firm of soul be faithful to me

In fair or in foul weather.
Walk on before me and do not look back.
And whatever lies ahead
Will be revealed to you by faith alone.
All this I swore. Loving, I promised
That I'd erect my universal house out of you,
That all the earthly lands would glorify you,
That out of the seed of your descendants,
Peace and salvation for all earth's peoples would come."
(January 1886)

32.

Mistress-Earth! To thee I bent my brow
And through thy fragrant veil
I felt the flame of a kindred heart,
I heard the trembling of cosmic life.
The grace of the shining heavens descended
In noonday beams of burning splendor,
And both the free-flowing river and the forest of many noises
Brought their melodious welcome to the quiet light.
And in clear sacrament I see again combined
The earthly soul and the unearthly light.
And, through the fire of love, the suffering
Of everyday life is borne away like fleeting smoke.
(May 1886)

33.

Oh heavy dream! In a mob of speechless visions,
Crowding and swarming round me,
I vainly seek the grace-giving shadow
That once did touch me with its wing.

But the moment I succumb to cruel doubts,
By an obscure anxiety and terror seized,
I sense above me once again the wings
Of the invisible shadow, hear again its words.

Oh heavy dream! The speechless mob of visions
Is growing, growing, blocking my pathway.
And I can barely hear the shadow's distant voice:
"Distrust the momentary. Love and don't forget!"
(1885, June 1886)

34.

In the Alps

Of wordless thoughts and feelings without name
A joyfully powerful tide.
A shaky embankment of hopes and of desires
Has all been washed away by a sky-blue wave.

Blue mountains press in all around;
The blue sea lies some distance off.
The wings of the soul rise high above the earth,
And yet they will not abandon earth.

Upon the shores of hope and of desire
The joyfully powerful tide
Splashes in pearly waves
Of wordless thoughts and feelings without name.
(August 1886)

35.

Taking an Autumn Road

Day fades. Above the exhausted, withered earth
The clouds, immobile, hang. Under the golden foliage
Of autumn that now bids farewell
One can discern both birches and lime trees.
Dreams gently sorrowful embrace the soul;
The infinite horizons stand there frozen.
And, reconciled, the heart does not long for
The sumptuously brilliant, noisy spring.
And it is as if the earth, in settling to its rest,
Has been immersed within a wordless prayer
And a pale-winged swarm of wordless spirits,
Invisible, from heaven on high descends.
(Autumn 1886)

36.

The fatal denouement of joyless love!*
Not quiet sorrow, but the hour of death's agony...
Life may be merely cruel deception, but the heart, in dying,
Languishes and aches, and on paradise's threshold
Yet burns with the fire that's gone out in eternity.
(1 January 1887)

37.

My friend! In olden times, as now,†
Adonis was being buried.
Moans and wailing filled the desert.
Sorrowing women wept.

* A poem inspired by Solovyov's love for Sophia Khitrovo.—ED.
† Addressed to Sophia Khitrovo.—ED.

My friend! In olden times, as now
Adonis rose from the grave.
Sightless malignity of hostile powers
Could pose no menace to his holiness.

My friend! Now, as in olden times,
We have interred our love,
But from far off the rays of love
Grow red again like a vermilion dawn.
(3 April 1887)

38.

Poor friend, the arduous path has exhausted you.
Your gaze has dimmed, and crumpled is your wreath.
Come to me to find your rest.
The sunset has burned low and has grown dim.

Where you have been and whither you are going,
Poor friend, I'll not inquire, loving you.
But you need only call my name and I
Will silently enfold you to my heart.

Death and Time reign over all the earth—
But do not call them sovereign.
And all things, whirling, vanish into darkness.
Only the sun of love remains at rest.
(18 September 1887)

39.

Not by fate's will, not by the thought of people,
Nor by your thought have I come to love you,

And by my prophetic love
I have protected you, I've rescued you
From spite invisible, from secret snares.

Let storm clouds gather round,
Let storms blow sinister and thunder sound.
Don't be afraid! The shield of my love
Will never falter even under darkest fate.
Between the celestial storm and you
It will still be standing, as before, unshakable.

And when before our eyes
Death puts out all the lights of earthly life,
The flame of the eternal soul, like the star from the East,
Will lead us toward the light that never fades.
And you will then be present before God,
Before the God of love, you'll be my answer.
(1890)

40.

Ex Oriente Lux[*]

"Light from the East, power from the East."
And, ready to assume total sovereignty,
The emperor of Persia chased
Herds of his slaves to Thermopylae.

But it was not in vain Prometheus'
Heavenly gift was given to Hellas.

* The light from the East refers to the appearance of Christianity. Solovyov yearned
for the unification of Western Catholicism and Eastern Orthodoxy, and nurtured the uto-
pian dream that all nations will unite fraternally in the spirit of Dostoevsky's "golden
age" (as described in the novel *The Adolescent*). Russia was to play a decisive role in this
unification, and Solovyov asks the question: "What kind of East do you (i.e., Russia)
wish to be? The East of Xerxes or the East of Christ?"—that is, a land of "eastern" des-
potism or a land that bears the universal principles of love?—ED.

Mobs of slaves run, growing pale,
Before a handful of valorous citizens.

And who was it that followed a glorious pathway
To the Indes and the Ganges?
The Macedonian phalanx first,
Then Rome's imperial eagle.

And by the power of reason and of law,
The universal principles of humankind,
The Empire of the West was thus erected,
And the world unified by Rome.

But what was lacking?
Why does the whole world lie in blood again?
The soul of the universe was longing
For the spirit of faith and love!

The prophetic word is not false.
The light shined from the East
And proclaimed and promised
What was impossible.

And, spreading far and wide,
Full of signs and powers,
The light that shined from the East
Has reconciled West with East.

O Russia! In the loftiest prophecy
You are preoccupied with a proud thought:
What kind of East do you wish to be?
The East of Xerxes or the East of Christ?
(1890)

[35]

41.

Heat without light, clouds that are moistureless,
Din of the city's daily grind...
Barren my thoughts within my yearning heart,
The trepidation of wingless reveries.

I am awaiting the arrival of a new cloud.
My thoughts will issue forth in tears,
And above that broken sorrowing your face
Will rise like the sun in its beams.
(1890?)

42.

It does not matter that a threatening crowd
Of darkening clouds has spread across the azure.
I see the lunar light—a light that's not removed
From earth by these clouds' heavy darkness.

It does not matter that a legion of life's ills
Has separated us once again.
Through the darkness from afar a power mysterious
Is sending me your quiet light.

The moon is silvering the borders
Of broken clouds with rays obscured.
Just one more instant and its face
Will shine above us in the azure.
(7 August 1891)

43.

*Nebuchadnezzar's Idol** *
Dedicated to K. P. Pobedonostsev†

He thus proclaimed to them: "My peoples!
All of you are slaves. I am the lord,
And from this time forth, from generation
To generation, let there be one god.

To the plain of Dura I summon you.
Let each reject his gods
And worship, rejoicing,
This creation of my hands."

Innumerable hordes of people swarmed
And the thunder rumbled out melodiously;
The priests obediently sang their hymns,
In front of the new altar bowing down.

And from Egypt to Pamir
The princes of the earth came to the call,
And they pronounced the man-made Idol
The Sovereign of Life.

It was magnificent, weighty, terrible.
The face of a bull, hindquarters of a dragon.
Above a pile of sacrificial offerings
It stood enveloped in incense.

And before the idol on the throne,
The holy sphere held in his hand,
Upon his head a crown of seven tiers,
Appeared Nebuchadnezzar.

---

* See Daniel 3–4.— ED.

† This poem was written in protest against the reactionary policies of Pobedonostsev (1827–1907), the right hand man of Tsar Alexander III. These policies helped to determine the course of the Russian Empire in the last quarter of the 19th century.— ED.

He made this declaration: "My peoples!
I am the king of kings, I am the earthly god.
Everywhere have I trampled upon freedom.
Before me has the earth grown silent.

But I have seen how you with brazenness
Have prayed to other gods, forgetting
That only he who is the king of the universe
Could be the giver of gods to slaves of his.

Now a new god has been given to you!
One that was consecrated by my imperial sword,
And for those who prove disobedient,
The cross and fiery furnace are prepared."

And savage wailings then were borne across
The plain: "You are the god of gods!"
They merged with the musical ringing
And the song of the tremulous priests.

Upon this day of madness and of shame
I called out mightily unto the Lord,
And louder than the sounds of that vile chorus
My voice resounded in the heavens.

And from the heights of Naharaim
The winds of a turbulent winter blew down.
And like the flame upon the altar,
The firmament opened above me.

And blizzards of whitest snow
With hail and with rain intermingling
Clothed all of the plains of Dura
Around in a crusting of ice.

The idol fell mightily
And lay there overturned.
And off in wildest agitation
The frightened people fled from it.

Where once the lord of the world had used to live,
I now saw shepherds.
And the creator of that idol
They set to graze amongst his herds.*
(Beginning of November 1891)

44.

At the wordless sunset hour
Remember those who have departed.
Whatever's been experienced with love
Has not then perished irretrievably.

Let bluing mists of night
Advance against the earth.
The night's obscurity has naught to frighten us:
The heart knows day is coming.

The Lord's new glory
Will illuminate the vault of heaven,
And down to the nether regions will
The radiant sounds of Sunday church-bells reach.
(1892)

* According to the Biblical story, Nebuchadnezzar was driven from human society
and ate grass like an ox (see Dan. 4:33). — ED.

45.*

....

Let early autumn have its laugh at me,
Let frost silver my temples and bedeck my head.
With a tremor of springtime do I stand before you,
All joyful and full of youthful yearning.

I've no wish to relinquish that dear image.
I've had enough of battle, striving, loss.
All life, which had become so difficult,
I think of now as a glorious fairy tale.
(January 1892)

46.

....

The way was hard and long. At least our gazes thrilled
At times to the bounty of miraculous nature.
But we were circled round by mountains unapproachable,
And my tired breast could barely catch its breath.

And suddenly roses began falling at sunset.
My soul became aware of two light wings,
And off to a new land of boundless reverie
Love, that enchantress, then transported me.

All silvered by moonlight is the meadow pure.
The trees like statues stand transfixed, and one
Catches sight of dancing swarms
Of gentle elves and of pale fairies gliding pensively.
(January 1892)

* Poems 45 to 53, dedicated to S. M. Martynova, with whom Solovyov was once infat-
uated, compose the so-called Martynova cycle, designed as a "romance in verse." Poems
47 and 48 are acrostics: SAFO (after Martynova's nickname).—ED.

47.

Something out of a fairy tale wafts in once more...
Angel or demon knocking at my heart. But which?
Frightened my feeling, now afraid to take a form...
Oh, how aware one is of cold words' impotence!
(3 January 1892)

48.

Strange whisper of unearthly words.
Aroma of Japanese roses...
Fantastical and misty,
Oh, echoing of springtime reveries.
(Between 3 and 15 January 1892)

49.
On the Occasion of the Two of Us Falling from a Sleigh

The sun was laughing high above us,
And you, my sun, were laughing too.
Having together shared this tumble,
What now remains for us is to share love.

I've rescued you from getting soiled,
Spreading myself out between you and the dirt.
So, my angelic one, in the same way,
Believe that I will shield you from all evil.

At the door you told me to leave,
But still you have remained within my heart,
And everything around me felt so light,
And the sun kept on laughing!
(26 January 1892)

50.
What Do People Live By?

People live by God's caresses,
Which pour invisibly down upon them.
They live by God's word, that silently
Within the universe resounds.

People live by the love
That draws all things together,
That triumphs over death
And will not cease in hell.

And when, without much boldness,
I think myself a part of "people," then
I live by the thought that my darling
And I will be together in eternity.
(30 January 1892)

51.

Three days I have not seen you, dearest angel.
Three eternities of torment lie ahead!
The universe to me seems but a grave,
And the life fades in my exhausted breast.

And I, a madman, sang that sorrow was over,
That love belated bears nothing but blossoms...
Everything sank at once in my crushed soul,
And from my radiant dream the wings were torn.

O darling! All of his proud consciousness,
His proud words would your friend at once give up
For but a fleeting moment of one meeting with you,
For the mere sound of the beloved steps.
(31 January 1892)

52.

I was magnificent. The earthly crowd
Swarmed somewhere down below me in the dust.
I alone stood there up above,
In company of the God of heaven and earth.

But where are the mountain peaks?
Where are the radiance and the thunder?
I lie here, on the valley floor,
In mute and saddened languidness.

O, how everything's been changed by love.
I wait, remaining motionless in the dust,
I wait for someone's little foot
To crush me with my grandeur.
(Between 31 January and 3 February 1892)

53.

I'm not afraid of death. There is no need for life now.
I am no longer needed by the empress of my thoughts.
No mortal love will bring her any comfort,
Nor can my clumsy verse give words to her.

But my eternal spirit, potent, free
Will find invisible anchorage in her breast,
Creating in her heart many sweet harmonies,
Encircling her soul with radiant dreams.

Nor will my spirit leave her for an instant.
It will illumine her with love eternal,
And melt with holy fire the dark element.
And painlessly from earthly fetters will free her.
(3 February 1892)

54.

Memory

Speed me along, o memory, on your ageless wing
Into the country dearest to my heart.[*]
I see her solitary there against the smoldering
Of fire in the winter twilight.

My soul is torn apart by bitter anguish.
There were two lives that turned to ashes there.
Something new is beginning far away
To take the place of spring that has perished.

Further along, O memory! With your wing
Gently fluttering blow another image to me...
I see her now upon a greening meadow
In the radiant summer.

The sun plays up above the wild Tosna,
High is the steep shore...
I see the old familiar pine trees,
The loose white sand...

O Memory, enough! All sorrows that I've felt
Again have seized possession of my soul.
As if those tears of all the former times
Are pouring forth now as a resurrected wave.
(29 February 1892)

* A reference to Pustynka, the estate belonging to S.A. Tolstaya, where most of Solovyov's romance with Sophia Khitrovo was played out. At the beginning of 1892, a fire had consumed the old house in Pustynka. "Something new is beginning far away" could be a reference to the romance with Martynova. The Tosna is the river that flowed past Pustynka. — ED.

55.

*Immanuel**

Into the darkness of the ages had the night
Receded when, worn out with evil and care,
The earth found rest in heaven's arms
And God-with-us was born in the stillness.

There is much that is now not possible:
No longer do kings look up at the sky
And shepherds do not listen in the desert
To the angels speaking about God.

But the eternal that had been revealed that night
Is that which cannot be destroyed by time,
And, born long ago in the manger, the Word
Has once again been born within your soul.

Yes! God is with us—but not there in the azure
Cave, nor beyond the numberless worlds.
Not in the evil fire, not in agitated breathing,
Not in the dormant memory of the ages.

He is *here and now*. Amidst our random vanities,
Within the confused stream of life's anxieties
You possess a secret wholly joyous:
Evil is powerless. We are eternal. God is with us!
(11 March 1892)

56.

Wind from the western land
Brings forth tears.

* See Matthew 1:23.—ED.

[45]

The sky is crying, the forest is moaning,
Its pine trees rocking.

From the land of the dead
Borne over to us comes a wailing.
The heart hears it and trembles.
The tears are gushing, gushing out.

The wind from the west has abated.
The sky is smiling.
But the heart has not returned
From the land of the dead.
(2 June 1892)

57.

Is it because my heart is compelled
To live by one thing, loving one thing?
Or because one who has not surrendered himself
Can never know delight?

Is it because fate has
Made our paths converge?
And because it is with you and you alone
That I could find happiness?

Is it because
In you, in you alone,
My heart, my life, and mind
Have drowned irretrievably?
(between 9 and 15 June 1892)

58.

Where willows like a family congregate,
And where a stream is breaking through,
There at the very bottom of the ravine,
Has the last nightingale begun to sing.

What does this signify? Renewal's joy
Or hopelessness of a farewell?
And far off in the distance there was movement
And the roaring of a train.

And the night sky towered,
In holy repose,
Above earthly love
And above earthly vanity.
(16 June 1892)

59.

Long have there been no questions, and no need of speech.
I rush toward you like a stream toward the sea.
Without doubt or thought I catch the dear image.
I know one thing alone: that I am mad with love.

I recognize you in dawn's scarlet shining.
In the light of heaven I see your smile.
And if it is my fate to die without you,
Yet will I shine, a brilliant star above you.
(17 June 1892)

60.

Too small, I see, is your heart for me.
Yet if I broke it I would still be sad.
If you only had a spark, just one, of living fire,
You cold, malicious siren!

But to forsake you or forget I have no power.
The world would then lose all its coloration,
And on that black night all mad songs
And fairy tales would forever cease to be.
(17 June 1892)

61.

Why words? In the azure boundlessness
Of ethereal waves, harmonious streams
Carry toward you the turbulent flame of desires
And the secret sighing of mute love.

And, trembling at the precious threshold,
A swarm of forgotten reveries rushes toward you.
The airy road isn't far away.
Just a single instant—and I am before you.

And at that instant of unseen encounter,
Again will the unearthly light illumine you,
And, sorrowing and loving, you will shed
The arduous dream of everyday consciousness.
(Beginning of September 1892)

62.

You and I were brought together
Not by chance. And it's not by chance
That my passion's like a fire.
These fiery torments
Are but the true signs
Of the power of being.

Into the abyss of darkness
Eternal love pours
Its living jet of fire.
From the flaming dungeon
I will again retrieve for you
The feather of the Fire-bird.

Light out of darkness.
The visages of your roses
Could not have risen above
The black of earth
If their dark roots
Had not sunk down
Into the dusky womb.
(15 September 1892)

63.

I have won the wished-for freedom,
Which lured me from afar like treasure.
But why do I feel an unexpected sorrow?
Why is it that this freedom does not please me?

My heart aches and my hands drop. Since
The fateful moment of our separation,
My cruel, my sweet friend,
Everything is so dim and lonely all around me.
(3 December 1892)

64.

Modest Prophecy

God's eye has turned toward summer.
But the frosts on earth get harsher.
Though you are cruelly cold to me,
I sense, I sense the fragrance of the rose.

My enemies have raised me to the rank
Of prophet—that's their way of mocking me.
But I am a true prophet in all that touches you,
And soon my prophecy will be fulfilled.

I prophesy—O listen to me, dryad!—
That snow will melt, cold pass, and that the earth,
Resurrected, will be joyous at the sun,
The woods will awaken and be as young as before.

I prophesy—this entre nous—that you
Will take your strolls in the garden
And take in with your nostrils and your eyes
The radiant consolation of May nights.
(10 December 1892)

65.

My dear friend, can it be
You do not see that all that we see

Is only a reflection, a mere shadow
Of what eyes do not see?

My dear friend, can it be
You do not hear that the vain din
Of daily life is only a distorted
Echo of triumphant harmonies?

My dear friend, can it be
You do not sense that all that matters
In this world is what heart says
To heart in wordless greeting?
(1892)

66.

I see your emerald eyes. Your image
Rises, luminous, before me. Into
These waking dreams which have no reveille
I have been borne by a new wave.

You languish, all entangled in the spiderweb
Of earth, my poor friend.
But have no fear: I'll not desert you—
It is closed, the magic circle.

Into these waking dreams which have no reveille,
We will be borne by a certain wave.
I see your emerald eyes,
Your luminous image is present to me.
(1892)

67.

The day has been one of merciless busyness
But now, surrounded by mild quietude,

You alone, O one miraculously beautiful,
You alone rule like an empress in my soul.

All the rebellious impulses and feelings,
The cruel life that seethed so in my blood,
Were swallowed up by an infinite striving
For a fateful, a consuming love.

The daytime moon, like a pale little cloud,
Barely glimmers in its whiteness,
But at night before it, all-triumphant one,
The sparks of the celestial fires fade.
(1892)

68.

O, what do all the words and speeches mean,
The ebb and flow of all these feelings,
In view of the unearthly mystery of our meeting,
In view of fate, fixed and eternal?

In this world of falsehood, O, how false you are!
Among deceptions, you are a living deception.
But it stays with me, it is mine, that happy moment
That will dissipate the fog of earth.

Let it be you don't believe in that meeting.
It doesn't matter—I'm not arguing with you.
O, what do all words and speeches mean
Before fixed, eternal fate?
(1892)

69.

Dear friend, I do not trust
Your words, feelings, or eyes.
And I do not trust myself. I trust only
The stars that shine far up above us.

On a milky way these stars
Send truthful dreams
And grow unearthly flowers for me
In an unending desert.

Amidst these flowers, in that eternal summer,
Glazed with azure silver,
How beautiful you are, and in the stellar light
How free and pure love is!
(1892)

70.
On the deck of the Torneo*

Behold: the lunar sickle has grown pale.
And Aphrodite's star has grown pale.
There on the wave's crest is a new reflection.
O wait together with me for the sun!

Behold how streams of blood
Flood the dark power.
The ancient warfare starts to rage again...
The sun, the sun's been vanquisher once more!
(28 July 1893)

* Written in Stockholm, where Solovyov spent the night on the deck of the ship Torneo, awaiting the sunrise. Poems 70–72 refer to a trip Solovyov made to Sweden. — ED.

71.

*On the road to Upsala**

Wherever you look are stones,
Just stones and pines…
Why is it that this poor land
Lies so close to my heart?

Here, eternally in dispute with nature,
Man's spirit grows
And from the agitation of the sea
Sends out its challenge to the heavens above.

And amongst the obscure contours
Of such stony heights as these
In the glow of the northern lights
One sees the entryway to the spirits' realm.

It can't be accidental that
From the inception of the world
Out of Kashmir and from the midday seas
This land was populated by so many heroes.†
(2 August 1893)

72.

On the deck of the Fritiofa

I had time to whisper just one single name
After the star that rolled down into the sea.
No time to make a wish; indeed, all wishing time is past
And all has faded—both happiness and sorrow.

* Written preparatory to a trip to Upsala, Sweden.—ED.
† This refers to the hypothesis, popular at the end of the 19th century, that the Germanic and Slavonic peoples had their origin in India.—ED.

[54]

Long time ago the shoreline disappeared.
A lone abyss of sea is the horizon.
My solitary soul contains the same unbounded
Expanse that lies all around me—before me and behind.
(6 August 1893)

73.

*A Moonlit Night in Scotland**
Dedicated to the Memory of Count F.L Sollogub†

Over the valley between mountain peaks,
A lunar ray has crept in through my window.
Outside, outside with you!
There is no way for one to get some sleep.

Brighter than a radiant dream, awake
The whole of the valley lies aglow.
I call on no one, no one to come with me.
Let only the waterfall speak.

Higher, higher, to where a solitary fir
Stands there above a cliff, where like
A spirit invisible a spring runs between the rocks,
Where gnomes live underneath the earth.

Wider, wider grows the horizon,
Clearer and clearer under the moon
Are the gray contours of the mountains
Reflected in the Lomond wave.

Why is the beauty of this night
Sad as a wordless phantom?
The heavens shed a cold light
And the earth is cold as the moon.

---

* This poem was written at Loch Lomond in Scotland. To it is appended a lengthy extract (not reproduced here) from Walter Scott's *Lady of the Lake.*—ED.

† F.L. Sollogub, amateur poet and artist, was a friend of Solovyov's.—ED.

It is as if a brilliant canopy
Stretches above the graves of ages past,
As if, this moonlit night, I am alone
On earth in an invisible crowd of the dead.

The lunar cold that seeps through all around
Pierces my soul...
But what is it that's suddenly shaken
The immobility of quietude?

Voices from invisible lands,
An unheard series of wild sounds.
A horn wails and a drum thunders,
And flutes whine furiously.

The solitary fir has come to life
And its branches make a noise that greets us.
The silent cliff has come to life as well.
The moss-covered granite is in a state of tremulous mystery.
(August 1893)

74.
A Parting with the Sea

Again and again I come with a lover's yearning
To suck in your infinitude with greedy eyes.
To you, too, my luminously green friend, must I say farewell.
Together, sea, we grumble, but I will not
Add to the salt water with my tears.

Upon my solitary winter way I'll take with me
This vital movement, voice, and coloration.
On sleepless nights, enchanting me with far off beauty,
You will remind me of your unforgettable caresses.
(1 November 1893)

75.

Happy New Year [1 January 1894]

The new year encounters graves that are new.
Too narrow for the past is new life's circle.
The joyous word will sound out dejectedly.
Nevertheless, my old, poor friend, Happy New Year!

Whether some fateful power or our infirmity
Has clothed radiant love in cruel passion,
Let us be thankful: the cup has passed us by.
Passion has burned itself out. We are free again.

If only time, having abolished our slavery,
Would not, too, rob our loving hearts of strength.
If only the specter of life unfulfilled
Would not peer into the soul like a living corpse.
(The end of November 1893).

76.

If desires flee like shadows,
If promises are empty words,
Is it worth living in this dark of error?
Is it worth living if the truth be dead?

Does one need eternity for vain strivings?
Does one need eternity for deceptive words?
That which is worthy of life lives without doubting.
The higher power cannot know any fetters.

Being conscious of a higher power in oneself,
Why should one still be yearning for childish dreams?
Life's but an exploit—and the living truth
Shines out immortally in rotting graves.
(1893?)

77.

*In the Vicinity of Abo**

Never will I forget you,
Beauty of this midnight land,
Where, loving the pale sky,
The sky-blue wave grows pale;
Where boundless winter night
Hides magic charms to suddenly raise
Within the white darkness
An intense flame—auroras of prophecy.
I wandered there in silence,
Where to the God of truth
I prayed that the tide of coercion would
Be smashed against the Finnish rocks.
(beginning of January 1894)

78.†

Skhodnia‡—An ancient road...
A new feeling, however, in my soul.
Fall in the background. There's so much
Omitted from the past!
(21 August 1894)

79.

Mon-repos

Gray sky and sea that's gray as well
Through gold and purple leaves.
It is as if a ponderous old grief's
Grown silent in its last autumnal adornment
Of luminous, transparent, radiant dreams.
(26 September 1894)

80.

Sorcerer-Rock
Dedicated to L. M. Lopatin[*]

These massive rocks, moss-covered,
Pull at the heart magnetically.
What could it be they need from mortals?
What mystery lies therein?

As an old legend would have it,
Gray-haired sorcerers
Have been transformed into these rocks
As punishment meted out by fate
For deeds most horrible.

They sleep in mute inaction.
But just one of these rock-men,
Once every aeon, rises, in his turn,
Up from his state of stupor.

His gray beard is sticking out,
His gaze afire, like a wolf's.
And, as he starts to breathe,
His mighty breast starts heaving.

* Lopatin (1855–1920), a well-known philosopher, was a childhood friend of Solovyov.— ED.

An invocation reverberates.
The surrounding dark is shaken.
And with a moan the Finnish wave
Beats against the coastline of the sea.

The storm wails. It roars and rumbles.
The sea has risen like a wall.
And farther off loud laughter
And the sorcerer's curse are heard.

The power of hellish breath
Has lifted all the deep.
Creatures of sin are perishing.
Deeds of sin are perishing.

And having carried out its destiny,
The prophetic rock's gone back to sleep.
But over it—pledging forgiveness—
A little star is shining quietly.

These massive rocks, moss-covered,
Pull at the heart magnetically.
What could it be they need from mortals?
What mystery lies therein?
(27 September 1894)

81.
*Panmongolism!**

Panmongolism! Although the word
Is strange, it caresses my hearing,
As though it were filled
With premonition of some mighty Divine fate.

* This poem, one of Solovyov's most famous, refers to the historiosophic conception
according to which the role of the leader of Christendom successively passed from Rome

When in corrupt Byzantium
The divine sanctuary had grown cold
And the Messiah had been renounced
By priest and prince, people and emperor—

He raised from the East
A people foreign and obscure,
And beneath fate's harsh arsenal,
The second Rome declined into the dust.

From the fate of fallen Byzantium
We do not seem to wish to learn,
And Russia's flatterers keep repeating:
You are The Third Rome. You are the Third Rome.

Let it be so! The arsenal of
God's punishment has not yet been exhausted.
Hordes of awakened tribes
Are making preparations for new onslaughts.

From the waters of Malaya to Altai,
The leaders from the eastern islands
Have gathered their multitudinous regiments
Together at declining China's walls.

As infinite as locusts,
And as insatiable as they,
Protected by an unearthly power,
The tribes march to the north.

O Russia! Forget the glory of your past:
The two-headed eagle has been crushed,

to Constantinople to Moscow; and to the view that unless the Russian Church subjugates herself to the law of love and charity, instead of to the law of coercion, Russia herself will be crushed by the Divine wrath, in the form of the "yellow peril" (fear of which was quite pronounced in Solovyov's day). This poem had a marked influence on the ideas of Alexander Blok (cf. his poem "The Scythians").—ED.

And the shreds of your banners have been given
To yellow-skinned children for playthings.

He who could forget the testament of love
Will find himself humbled in fear and trembling...
And the third Rome lies in the dust.
There will not be a fourth.
(1 October 1894)

82.
Saimaa*

The lake splashes in agitated waves.
Just like the gathering tide of the sea,
Chaotic, the element rushes forth toward something,
Is arguing over something with a hostile fate.

The lake must hate its granite fetters!
Peace is a comfort only in what is measureless.
The lake is dreaming of past primordial ages.
It wishes once again to rule the land.

Struggle, bestir yourself, wild captive!
And everlasting shame on voluntary slaves.
Your dream will come true, O mighty element.
There'll be expanse enough for all your free waves.
(3 October 1894)

* Poems 82–84 refer to Saimaa, a Finnish lake. — ED.

83.

What was it that happened to you last night?
Did the angel of hope speak with you?
Or did the storm of yesterday wear you out,
And are you resting before some new battle?

Illuminated streams are gently prattling,
The heavens' grace is gently shining.
Far off, the bare trees make
A sudden noise and then grow quiet again.
(4 October 1894).

84.
*Dedicated to N.E. Auer**

This luminous expanse of pearl, like frosted glass,
Up in the heavens and in the mirror plain,
And, in the distance, this pattern of black transfixed —
Where the forest is reflected in the abyss.

If the transparent air sometimes brings
With it a child's cry or the bells of a herd,
Here, the very sounds sound out like quiet,
With no disturbance of the wordless delight.

O, to remain like this for ever —
Luminous and warm here on the clean unmelting snow.
Cruel memory and sorrow — all have gone somewhere,
All has vanished into this luxuriance's enchantment.
(11 October 1894)

* A female friend of Solovyov's. See also poem 94. — ED.

85.

I've come to love you, gentle beauty,
On luminously transparent and on somber days.
I love both your clear boundless gazes
And the stern shadow of your sad thought.

Can this unexpected caress be a deception?
And will you, too, deceive a pilgrim?
But my heart keeps saying: here's the wished-for harbor
At the feet of an untroubled holy beauty.

Love me, too, gentle beauty,
On luminously transparent and on somber days.
And may those clear and boundless gazes
Of yours dispel all past grief like a shadow.
(11 October 1894)

86.
Christmas Eve
Dedicated to V.L. Velichko

It may well be that the crimes of aeons
Have desecrated all things and naught's remained unsoiled.
But stronger than any doubt is conscience's reproach.
And what has once been kindled in the soul cannot fade.

That which is great has not occurred in vain.
It's not in vain that God appeared among men,
That sky bent down to earth, that portals of
The palace of the eternal have been flung open.

Within depths of the cosmic consciousness invisible,
Unsilenced dwells the source of truth.
And up above the ruins of ancient shame
Truth's word sounds out like a funereal ringing.

The light was born in the world, and the light was rejected by the
darkness.
But it shines in the darkness, at the boundary of good and evil.
Not by a power external but by truth itself
Are the prince of this age and all his works condemned.
(24 December 1984)

87.

Winter on the Saimaa[*]

In a thick fur you've wrapped yourself,
And lie there hushed in an untroubled sleep.
No breath of death here in the radiant air,
In this white quietude, transparent.

No, not in vain was it that I sought you
In this profound, unagitated stillness.
Before my inner eye your image rests unchanged,
O Fairy Queen, mistress of pines and cliffs!

You are immaculate, like the snow beyond the mountains.
You are filled with many thoughts, like the winter night.
You are all-radiant like the polar flame,
Most luminous daughter of dark chaos!
(December 1894)

88.

The distant noises of the cataract
Resound throughout the woods.
A quiet consolation is wafting in
From beyond the twilight heavens.

* See note to poem 82. — ED.

Only the white airy vault,
Only the white dream of earth...
The heart, obedient, has grown silent.
And all anxieties have passed.

Motionless consolation.
All things have merged as if in dream.
The distant noises of the cataract
Resound within the quietude.
(End of December 1894)

89.

To Departed Friends

I've barely left behind the agitation of daily life,
Yet my departed friends already have assembled in a crowd.
And distant visions of past obscure years
Are more and more distinctly here before me.

All earthly daylight suddenly fades and pales.
The soul is inebriated with sweet sorrow.
Though it is yet invisible, the spring is coming
With its sounds and its breath of the eternal.

I know: it's you, my friends, who've bent your gaze to the earth,
You who have raised me above careworn vanity,
Who have revived the memory of the eternal meeting,
So nearly washed away by waves of daily life.

I do not see you yet, but at the appointed hour,
When I pay full tribute to cruel destiny,
You'll open wide the place where reconciliation dwells
And show the pathway to the unfading stars.
(Mid-January 1895)

90.

Imatra[*]

Noise and alarm in a profound repose.
Turbid waves amid white snows.
The azure spot of the coastal ice.
The quiet veil of the sky of pearl.

Likewise, cosmic life in its agitated striving
Is borne in a turbulent stream.
The same immutable repose reigns
In the unceasing, though momentary, noise.

Do not catch, child, in your vain desire,
The wave of passion with its seething foam.
Look up above you at the potent, fixed,
And heaven-convergent shore of love.
(January 1895)

91.

To the memory of A. F. Aksakova[†]

Once more do the excruciating shades draw near
Of those the heart's forgotten and of faded dreams.
Knees bend in the face of the unknown
And streams of tears rush toward the irretrievable.

Not tears for the departed. No! They will return.
It is the moment gone forever that one misses.
It can't be resurrected, and the heavy years
Drag slowly on after the instant of eternity.

---

[*] Famous waterfall in Finland. — ED.

[†] A.F. Aksakova (1829–1889) was the wife of the Slavophile Ivan Aksakov and a friend of Solovyov's. — ED.

Or is such a thought deception, and does the past contain only
The shades of those the heart's forgotten and of faded dreams?
Knees bend in the face of the unknown
And streams of tears rush toward the irretrievable.
(January 1895)

92.

Dreaming while awake

An azure eye
Is gazing through the somber, threatening clouds...
Stepping deep,
Into this desert of crumbling snow,
Toward an enigmatic goal
I walk alone.
Only the firs are behind me;
And, far off,
A lake spreads itself wide in white adornment.
The silence tells me that the unexpected will soon occur.
The azure eye
Has sunk again into the mist.
Into solitary anguish
The hope for meeting fades.
Far off, the sorrowing firs,
Motionless, grow dark.
Desert without aim
And path without destination.
And, unreproachfully, that same voice sounds within the quiet:
The end is near. The unexpected will soon occur.
(January 1895)

93.

To the Resurrected

The young spring day sends us battalion
After battalion of brilliant rays.
But surreptitiously the massiveness
Of the ice is fortified by nighttime shadows.

Between patches of snow the earth is black.
Nevertheless the mourning gladdens us
When it is flooded with triumphant rays
Of the impending spring.

The soul's ripe blossoming will not
Be held back by a snow of graying locks.
The gaze of your eyes will light
This mix of wintertime and summer.
(16 April 1895)

94.

Dedicated to N. E. Auer

As soon as the shadow of the living, having glimmered, disappears,
The shadow of the dead is already at hand
And once again they're answered by
A bitter joy and by sweet sorrowing.

What can this presage for me, this insistent
And powerful summoning of kindred shadows?
A blossoming of fresh powers, clear
And triumphant? Or the end of mortal days?

But whatever it may mean, your salutation from
Beyond the grave, my heart beats in accord with it.
My heart is rushing after you, toward you, and on
This dusty road there is no way back.
(23 April 1895)

95.

Dedicated to Prince A.D. Obolensky

Finally she has shaken off
Her adornment all outmoded,
Has smiled and sighed,
And her clear gaze has opened.

The flaming roses of the sky
Are all reflected in the wave,
And the woods have spread the spirit of the birch
In a transparent semi-reverie.

Why is this day of blossoming
A day of sorrow for me?
Why is it that I bear the shadow
Of night to a festival of light?

Separated from an awakened earth,
In a mute land
Someone whispers with a heavy sorrow:
"Remember me."†
(28 April 1895)

* Obolensky, a government official, was a friend of Solovyov's.—ED.
† Solovyov was thinking of his great friend, the deceased poet Fet.—ED.

96.

The threatening powers that had thundered at midday
Have dissipated, long ago exhausted...
Behold: the meek stars up above are shining
And looking quietly into the window.

But silent flashes keep on telling the tired earth
About the storm it had experienced,
And on this night of sleeplessness the earth
Does not believe that the desired peace will come.
(1895)

97.
June night on Saimaa*

On this gold-purple night
We'll clearly not remain alone.
Through the roses of the heavens I caught
Something of withheld turbulence in your gaze.

And here midnight has imperceptibly passed by...
Above you it grows lighter and lighter still,
But the cherished holiness that rules
My destiny has faded.

I am not captivated by the power of the sun
But I grow cold whenever I look at you!
A certain word is whispering in secret
To my sorrowful soul.

I know that one pallid morning of autumn,
I know that one icy winter sunset,

* See poems 82–84, 87.

[71]

This triumphant word will sound out,
And you will repeat it after me!
(17 June 1896)

98.

Thunderstorm in the morning

The pealing of the thunder has chased off
The gathering flock of obscure words.
Before the fiery-violet abyss
The veil has been torn to the verge.

The ripe streams noisily pour forth;
The thunder roars as if being comforted by something…
I see your darkened eyes,
Though curtained off from you by rain.

Suddenly it's grown silent… Someone is bidding farewell.
And apertures are opening out into the azure…
But your gaze is two-fold: it smiles, but it grows dark
As well with this so unforgettable tempest.
(18 June 1896)

99.

On a train in the morning.
*Dedicated to V. P. Gaideburov**

Fresh air and a window, won after battle…
A yellow birch between dark firs,
And beyond them the light-blue sky
And the soft beds of future grains.

* Gaideburov was a poet. — ED.

With phantom breath the noisome locomotive
Rushes ahead and rumbles with dead thunder,
While nature's soul in hushed caress
Lies transfixed up above in motionless brilliance.

Is there no end of this painful breach?
Or will imaginary strife be vanquished and
The soulless locomotive then converge with this
Immobile life at some beneficent destination?
(September 1896)

100.
To a friend of youth.
*For Prince D. N. Tsertelev**

Of all these grand and clever conversations,
I am an enemy,
An enemy, too, of all the barren noisiness
Of endless disputation...

....

Do you remember when—
Those nights were long ago—
The dawn from the east
Greeted us with its quietude?

From briefest hints,
Opening to the depths of life,
A fateful mystery
Silently arose.

---

* The poet Prince Dmitry Nikolaevich Tsertelev (1851–1911) was a friend of Solovyov's from the beginning of the 1870's and was in Egypt together with Solovyov in 1876 at the time of Solovyov's great vision of Sophia. — ED.

What we could not put
In final form at that time—
Eternity has inscribed
On obscure tablets.
(End of December 1896).

101.

No one can lift by force the heavy veil
Of the gray heavens.
Far off, the same little path winds its way,
And it is the same forest.

And in the depths, a question, one sole question
Was posed by God.
O, if only you could answer it at least with
A swan song!

The whole world is a frozen dream,
As it was on the first day.
The soul is alone, and sees in front of itself
Its own shadow.
(1897)

102.
To the memory of A. A. Fet

He was an old man, long-sick and frail.
How long he kept on living filled us
With amazement. But time—
Why can't it reconcile me with his grave?

He did not bury his gift of mad songs in the earth.
All that his spirit commanded him to say he said.
Why has he not grown bodiless to me,
And his gaze not grown pale within my soul?

There is a mystery here... I hear someone calling
And a baleful moaning with a tremulous plea...
What's left unreconciled is sighing like an orphan,
And what is solitary mourns itself.
(16 January 1897)

103.

The Eye of Eternity
"Thou shalt have no other gods before me." (Exodus 20:3)

Alone, alone above white earth
Burns the star
And draws one far by an ethereal pathway
To itself—up there.

O no! Why? A single, fixed gaze
Contains all miracles.
Both the mysterious sea of all life
And the heavens above.

This gaze is so close and so clear.
Look into it—
And you yourself will grow boundless and beautiful,
The king of all that is.
(16 January 1897)

104.

*On the death of A. P. Maikov**

The ancient shadows that confine the soul
In ringing crystals now are quietly departing.
Many are still being called to the realm of song
But now there are almost none being chosen.

Prophetic witnesses of a life lived out,
You have eternalized all that shined in life.
Beneath your flowers the hidden fruit of earth
Has grown, and a new seed secretly has ripened.

Ancient shadows, peace to you with love!
Let the pure crystals sparkle as before,
So as, sweetly ringing in the realm of song,
To call forth to the future what has passed.
(9 March 1897)

105.

For A. A. Fet
(Dedication to a book about the Russian poets)†

All threads are torn, all echoes silent, but
The key to hidden joy has stayed within the soul,
And in the soul a certain ray mysterious, unchanging
Will not fade before the eternal meeting.

And within this realm of error, I would enter
With that ray into the crucible of prophetic dreams,
To crown the singers who have fallen silent
With the reflection of immortal revelations.

---

* A celebrated poet (1821–1987).— ED.

† This poem was evidently intended as a dedication to a collection of Solovyov's essays, *Russian Lyrical Poetry in the Nineteenth Century*, a work which never appeared.— ED.

Departed friend! Beforehand I have had
Your blessing of this pathway.
I hear the Imperceptible approaching,
And an invisible tide finds entry to my heart.
(July 1897)

106.
To an old friend
*For A. P. Salomon**

When we were in our twenties, supreme fate
Ordained that we two would share both joys and worries.
Could it be that, for all the rest of our road,
The flow of mundane life will separate us?

Confined within the dungeon of the corruptible world
And paying tribute to the vanity that reigns,
Within the hidden chapel we are free
Not to betray the sublime dream we had.

Let it perish, all that does not withstand truth
But we will preserve eternity's pledge,
Pledge of what secretly is sought by the immortal spirit,
Of what the immortal God has clearly promised.
(July 1897)

107.

I am illuminated by the smile of autumn.†
It is dearer than the heavens' bright laughter.

---

* See note to poem 31.—ED.
† Written in Sophia Khitrovo's estate Pustynka and inspired by memories of Solovyov's love for her.—ED.

From within a formless, shifting crowd
A ray gleams forth—and just as suddenly vanishes.

Weep, autumn, weep. Your tears are comforting!
Trembling forest, send your sobbing to the sky!
Roar, storm, roar out all your threats,
Exhausting them upon the breast of earth!

Mistress of the earth, of the heavens and sea!
I can hear you even through this somber moaning,
But here your gaze, disputing with the hostile darkness,
Was suddenly lit by the celestial dome that had grown light.
(26 August 1897)

108.
The native land of Russian poetry
With reference to Zhukovsky's translation of Gray's "Elegy."
For P. V. Zhukovsky[*]

Not where the coastal granite has enchained broad Neva
In immobile armor, or where the tall Kremlin, witness of
The storms of olden times, stands silent
Above motley Moscow did Russian poetry arise.

Rather it arose 'mid changeless birch and pine trees
Peering from earth's darkness into heaven,
"Where the village elders lie in solitary graves,"
Crowned with crosses, sleeping the sleep of the exhausted.

There, at sunset, in the autumn,
This sorceress was born into the world,
And the woods received her with their fallen foliage,
And quietly rustled with their sorrowful greeting.

* The great poet V. A. Zhukovsky's (1783-1852) translation of Thomas Gray's "Elegy
Written in a Country Graveyard" is considered to be one of the finest poetic translations
into Russian. P. V. Zhukovsky (1840-1912), V. A. Zhukovsky's son, was an artist. — ED.

And to the secluded cradle, strict songs
Were carried from beyond the sea, from misty isles,
But having gathered at the cradle, they sang so gently
Over the prophetic silence of the fathers' graves.

It was not by chance that at the village graveyard,
You appeared, O sweetest genius of my native land!
And ever after you've enchanted us with a rainbow
Of dreams, with the heat of youthful passion,
But the first and the best gift of all
Was that sorrow with which God filled you
In autumn there in the old graveyard.
(12 October 1897)

109.
Response to "Songs from a 'corner'"
For K. K. Sluchevsky[*]

Your verses' evening light
Gifts me with double comfort:
With thought's pellucid coolness
And with that which bears no name.

What an autumn! Strange it is that
With neither hot spells nor turbulent storms,
Yet from the equinox your day
Has not decreased but has only grown longer.

Let it be shining thus even in winter.
When there's no longer strength to shine,
Let it shine forth with a prophetic dawn,
A dawn that lasts through the entire mute night.
(January 1898)

[*] A well-known poet (1837–1904) who was highly valued by Solovyov. — ED.

110.
*The Sign**

> *"her seed... shall bruise thy head..."*
> (Genesis 3:15)

> *"...he that is mighty hath done to me great things; and holy is his name."*
> (Luke 1:49)

> *"And there appeared a great wonder [sign] in heaven; a woman clothed with
> the sun, and the moon under her feet, and upon her head a crown of twelve
> stars." (Rev. 12:1)*

Alone! Forever alone! Let there be hellish brilliance
In the darkness and thunder amid the quiet in the sleeping temple.
No matter that all around us has fallen. The banner alone
Will not tremble nor the shield move from the destroyed wall.

In slumberous horror we ran to the sanctuary
And the suffocating burning filled the temple.
Fragments of silver lay all scattered
And black smoke clung to the tattered carpets.

And only the sign of the incorruptible covenant
Was present, as before, between heaven and earth.
And from heaven, the selfsame light illumined both
The Virgin of Nazareth and the poisonous serpent powerless
    before her.
(March 1898)

* This poem is linked with Solovyov's eschatological yearnings, which intensified
toward the end of his life. It was a favorite poem of the Russian symbolists. The occasion
for the writing of the poem was an explosion in a church in the Kursk monastery. — ED.

111.

*In the Archipelago at Night**

No, don't believe in the spell-induced deception
That the intermeshing of dead powers
Could cause God's creation to perish,
That blind destiny could threaten us.

In mists of the sea I have borne witness
To the entire play of hostile charms.
The sinister vapor was intent on killing me
Not just in some illusion but in fact.

Legions of spirits of hell
All took on form and then rose up,
And combinations of malicious words
Resounded piercingly.

The material world is all deception.
Dark vapors there breathe with a raging fury...
Within the mists of the sea I have borne witness
To the malevolent power of hostile charms.
(8–11 April 1898)

112.

Das Ewig-Weibliche †
Word of Admonishment to the Sea Demons

The demons of the sea have fallen in love with me.
They've been chasing me like bloodhounds.
They tried to catch me off the Finnish coast.
To the Archipelago I went—they were already there!

---

* Solovyov wrote poems 111-115 while sailing the Mediterranean during his second
trip to Egypt.— ED.

† Das Ewig-Weibliche (the Eternal Feminine) is borrowed from Goethe's *Faust*.—
ED.

Clearly, these demons want to see
Me dead: that's in the nature of demons.
God be with you, demons! But take my word
For it, I will not let you eat me.

You would be better off were you to heed
My words. I've kind advice to give to you:
Dear demons, you can, if you wish to do so,
Become God's little creatures once again.

Do you remember how at the sea where once
Stood Amaphunt and Paphos[*]
You chanced to experience
The first unexpected sorrow of your lives?

Do you recall the roses above the white foam,
The purple reflection in the azure waves?
Do you recall the form of the beautiful body,
Your confusion, trepidation, and fear?

That beauty with its initial force
Could not long, demons, keep you terrified.
It tamed your savage malice for the moment
But could in no way conquer it.

Into that beauty, O demons full of cunning,
You soon found a secret pathway for yourselves.
And the hellish seed of corruption and
Of death you sowed within that beautiful form.

But know this: the eternal feminine
In incorruptible body is now coming to the earth.
In the unfading light of the new goddess
Heaven has merged with the watery abyss.

* Ancient cities on Cyprus. — ED.

All that makes the earthly Aphrodite beautiful:
The joy of homes, forests, and seas—
Will be included in the unearthly beauty
More purely, strongly, vitally, and fully.

In vain do you seek to approach her!
Clever demons, why make such a din?
That which nature waits for with yearning
You can neither delay nor subjugate.

Proud demons—you are nevertheless men,
And it does a man no honor to quarrel with a woman.
And so, if only for this reason, dear demons,
You should surrender, and be quick about it!
(8-11 April 1898)

113.
Past Troy

Something has been orphaned here,
Someone's lamp has ceased to shine,
Someone's joy has flown away,
Someone was singing—but now he's fallen silent.
(Between 11 and 14 April 1898).

114.
The Nile Delta

Golden, emerald,
Black-earth fields...
Much-laboring, silent land,
There's nothing tightfisted about you!

This fruitful womb,
How many sleepy ages
Did it receive, ever-obedient,
Both seeds and corpses.

But not all that you received
Did you bring forth each year:
What is bewitched by ancient death
Still waits for spring.

It is not Isis of the three crowns
Who will bring that spring to them,
But the immaculate, eternal
"Virgin of the Rainbow Gates."*
(14 April 1898)

115.
Song of the Sea
For A. A. Fet

From whom has this warm southern sea
Learned the bitter songs of cold seas?
And beneath some other sky, in disputation with the inevitable,
The selfsame shadow† stands above my dream.

Or are the consonant sobs of the deep so insufficient for it
That it still wants tears from the constricted heart,
Another's tears, another's selfless mourning
Above a grave of reveries madly discarded...

What help for a deceiving, deceived lot?
How can the problem of fate be solved

* Solovyov uses this gnostic term in the sense of the Eternal Feminine or the World Soul. — ED.
† The deceased Fet. — ED.

For someone else? Who'll tell me? But the heart aches
With pain and can't forget another's downfall.

Splashes of life were fused in diamond reveries
But now, the moment that the radiant net shines,
The pearl that is your song dissolves in tears
To make lament and grumble with the deep.

The is the only song the southern sea knows,
Just like the agitated waves of the cold seas—
The song of grief that's foreign, distant, dead,
Which, like a shadow, is inseparable from my soul.
(April 1898)

116.
Answer to "Yaroslavna's Lament"*
For K. K. Sluchevsky

Everything, in changing, has produced change.
Everywhere there are the crosses on the graves,
But the testaments of creative reverie
Awake my soul as strongly as before.

The poet's eternal madness
Is like a cold spring amid the ruins…
Unheedful of time's prohibitions,
He alone preserves life in death.

Let it be so that Troy was long ago
Laid waste. Let the quiet Don have its peaceful slumber.
We hear the selfsame same grumbling of Andromache,
The selfsame moaning over Putivl.†

* A poem of Sluchevsky's (see note to poem 109).—ED.
† A city in Kievan Russia. In the great ancient poem "The Lay of the Host of Igor,"
Yaroslavna weeps on the wall surrounding Putivl.—ED.

One's own will not return.
The familiar words grow mute
And yet the memory of the distant past
Lives still in a transparency of tears.
(19 June 1898)

117.
Returning to the Same Place

*"And thou shalt remember all the way which the Lord thy God led thee
these forty years in the wilderness... And he humbled thee, and suffered
thee to hunger, and fed thee with manna... Thy raiment waxed not old
upon thee, neither did thy foot swell, these forty years."* (Deut. 8:2–4).

Gone are twelve years of consuming preoccupations,
Of torturous reveries and anxious cares,
Of temptations that would momentarily triumph but then fall away,
Of bitter inebriation and of sober toil.

Praise to the Eternal! Israel's raiment did He keep
Intact for forty years in the desert...
The best hopes lie intact in the soul:
The wellspring of its creative powers has not dried up.

O mistress earth! With the accustomed tenderness
And with such love do I bend over you.
The ancient woods and river resound for me with youthful song...
And all that is eternal in them has stayed with me.

True, that was a different day, cloudless and bright.
A stream of triumphant rays flowed from the heavens
And everywhere among the trees of the neglected park
I could catch phantom glimpses of your enigmatic eyes.[*]

[*] Solovyov remembers his love for Sophia Khitrovo.—ED.

The phantoms have departed, but my faith is unchanged...
Behold: All at once the sun peers from behind the clouds.
Mistress earth! Your beauty is incorruptible
And the radiant hero is both immortal and strong.
(29 June 1898)

118.

[11 June 1898]

A flock of clouds has gathered
There on the horizon and is growing...
On the dry lap of earth
All living things await the water of life.

But, wearisome, the stubborn
Wind chases the clouds.
The heat continues to torment us.
The water of life is somewhere far away.

Likewise, the hopes the soul possesses
Are chased away by noise of mundane life,
By anger's voice, the ignoramus' cry,
By the eternal wind of idle thoughts.
(May or June 1898)

119.

Ya. P. Polonsky * : *In memoriam*

The extinguished ray
Of the pale-tender light.
The sigh of coastal wind,
The land of distant storm-clouds...

---

* A well-known lyrical poet (1819–1898).

[87]

The heroism of the female heart,
The shadow of male evil,
The shining of the universal sun
And darkness of the earth...

That which tortures us at every instant
With painful rupture—
You perceived all this
With a transforming sense of what is beautiful.

A new path is stretching
Now before you. But nonetheless
Your heart will still look back
With quiet sorrowing.
(19 October 1898)

120.

The instant that you doze in daytime or wake up
At night someone is there... There are two of us.
Radiant eyes look straight into my soul
In dark night and in daytime.

The ice melts; somber storm-clouds all disperse.
The flowers are blooming...
And your reflection can be found in the
Transparent stillness of fixed harmonies.

Within my soul the old original sin is disappearing.
Through the mirrory smoothness
One cannot see the grass, discern
The sea-serpent, or make out the cliffs.

One sees only the light and water. And
In the transparent mist someone's eyes shine.
And long ago, like dew in the ocean stream,
All the days of our quotidian life were merged.
(21 November 1898)

121.

Two Sisters[*]
From an Icelandic saga
Dedicated to A.A. Lugovoi

The maiden Injury beats her wings
There, on the wild cliffs...
There is a black cloud up above us.
Our hearts contain alarm and fear.

The sorrowing maiden makes moan.
Quiet is her moaning on the earth.
A voice of threatening rage
Accompanies her up above there in the darkness.

A moan, reiterated by the thunder,
Travels far off to the distant stars,
Where between the gods and the earth
The maiden Punishment Eternal dwells.

There, where one sees the brilliant columns
Of the auroras of the midnight,
There she can be seen, the maiden of
Desires, the maiden of final destiny.

* The "Injury" here is that done to the Finnish nation by the Russian Empire. Alex-
ander Alekseevich Lugovoi (1853–1914), a writer, was a friend of Solovyov's.—ED.

Before her is a golden cup.
Dropping into the cup, like vapors
From the earth, dropping like large
Drops of dew, the tears of Injury fell.

Quietly, the powerful maiden
Quietly, wordlessly is seated.
Her fixed gaze is directed into
The cup of threatening rage.

There is a black cloud up above us.
Our hearts are filled with alarm and fear...
The maiden Injury beats her wings
There, on the wild cliffs.
(3 April 1899).

122.
Chez moi

The white nights are waiting here for me
Above the expanse of densely clustered islands...
The familiar eyes are gazing once again
And the past is glimmering wordlessly.

I still do not believe in time's dominion.
Still do I guard the power of the heart.
And I will not conceal the fateful loss,
Yet I cannot say "forever."

In the protracted glow of sunset,
Before the day has gone to sleep,
You'll not, this night, convince me that the light
Of day has faded never to return.
(June 1899)

123.

White Bellflowers
"And I hear how the heart blooms"
Fet

How many of them have recently been blooming.
As if they were a white sea in the woods!
Rhythmically a warm wind rocked them to and fro,
Protecting them in all their youthful beauty.

That beauty of theirs is fading, fading.
That wreath all snowy-white has now grown dark.
And now it seems to me as if the entire world
Is withering… And amid the graves I stand alone.

"We, your white thoughts, we all live by
The secret pathways of your soul. When you
Are wandering there along the somber road,
We motionlessly shine out in the stillness.

It is not the capricious wind that has protected us;
We would have saved you from the snowstorms.
Come to us quickly through the rainy west.
For you we are—the cloudless south.

If mist closes off sight
Or sinister thunder sounds,
Our heart blooms and sighs…
Come—and you'll learn what it's sighing for."
(15 August 1899)

124.

You dream a peaceful dream.
But we no longer believe in dreams.
Everywhere we hear only war cries.
Everywhere is the moment of death or victory.
(1890s?)

125.

Impenetrable darkness all around.
The rumbling of distant thunder.
There is no clearing in the night sky.
The stars have hid—don't wait for their return.
(1890s?)

126.
Les Revenants[*]

By a secret pathway, sorrowful and dear,
You have found a way to my soul, and thanks be to you!
It is sweet for me to approach with dejected memory
Death-shrouded, quiet shores.

By an incomprehensible thread my heart is still attached
To meaningless images, to weeping shadows.
Something asks to be put into words; something has been left unsaid.
Something is happening—though not here nor there.

Past moments with soundless tread have come up to me
And suddenly removed the veil from my eyes.

* Phantoms (French).—ED.

They see something eternal, something that does not depart,
And the past years as but a single hour.
(16 January 1900).

127.

The Dragon
*For Siegfried**

From out the circles of heaven invisible
Has the dragon shown his brow,
And the impending day has been veiled
By a darkness of invincible woes.

Will there now be no end to the exultations
And to the praise of the everlasting world,
To the carefree laughter and exclamations:
"Life is good; there is no evil in it!"

Heir of the sword-bearing host!
To the sign of the cross you are true.
There is Christ's fire in your sword,
And your terrible speech is holy.

The lap of God is full of love.
It calls us all alike... But before
The dragon's jaws we understand:
The cross and the sword are one.
(24 June 1900).

* This poem refers to the sending of troops by Emperor Wilhelm II (Siegfried) to
crush a rebellion in China. — ED.

128.

Again the White Bellflowers[*]

On fierce, on broiling
Summer days
They are the same:
Shapely and white.

Let the phantoms of spring
Be burned.
Here you are, unearthly,
Truthful dreams.

Evil once experienced
Sinks down into the blood.
The sun of love,
Washed-pure, rises up.

There are bold plans
Within the heart that's sick —
White angels
Have risen all around.

Shapely and airy,
They are just the same —
On heavy, suffocating
Days, fierce days.
(8 July 1900).

[*] Written just before Solovyov's death. — ED.

Parodies of the Russian symbolists[*]

1.

Vertical horizons
In the chocolate sky,
Like semi-mirror dreams
In cherry-laurel woods.

The fire-breathing ice-floe phantom
Has vanished in bright twilight.
And he stands there paying me no heed,
A hyacinth pegasus.

Immanent mandragoras
Are rustling in the reeds,
And the crunchily decadent verses
Resound in my withering ears.

2.

Above the green hill,
Above the hill that is green,
To us who are in love,
To us who are in love with each other,
A star shines at midday,
At midday it is shining,
And this though no one will ever
Take notice of that star.
But the undulating mist,
The mist that undulates,
From radiant lands,

* Solovyov carried on a running polemic in the 1890s with the emotionally and spiritually vague and vapid (in his opinion) Symbolist (or "decadent") poets like Valery Briusov and Konstantin Balmont, whom he parodies here. — ED.

[95]

From a radiant land,
It glides between the clouds,
Above the dry wave,
It is motionlessly flying
And it has a double moon.

3.

In the heavens the chandeliers burn.
But here down below—it's dark.
Did you see him or didn't you see him?
Inform us all right now!

But don't tease the hyena of suspicion
With the mouse of angst!
Don't look at how the leopards of vengeance
Are sharpening their teeth!

And the owl of prudence—do not call her out
Into this night!
The asses of patience and the elephants of reflection
All have run away.

You have given birth to the crocodile of your fate—
Without help from anyone else.
The chandeliers burn in the heavens
But within the graves—it's dark.
(summer-autumn 1895)

Undated Poems

a.

When into my dry field
I received a seed of truth,
It sprouted—and hurriedly
I gathered the first harvest.

But it was not I who nurtured this seed to growth,
Not I who gave it rain to drink,
Not I who blew the coolness upon it,
Not I who warmed it with brilliant ray.

O no! I crushed out all the crop
With thistles and with thorns.
I squeezed it and I stifled it
With the chaff of human strivings.

b.

My heart is singing an old song to me.
Before me dreams of old are resurrected.
Somewhere far off the flowers are blossoming,
The magical voice is sounding out and calling.

A marvelous fairy-tale is coming alive before me.
Against my will I once again believe in that fairy tale.
The heart feels so much sweetness and such pain.
An unearthly spring now breathes upon my soul.

c.

What's suddenly happened to you? Whence did you bring
That miraculous light that shines in your marvelous eyes?

Perhaps, its source is not to be found
In heavenly rays, nor here on earth...

But why are you looking like that? Why so keenly
Listening, seeing nothing and having forgotten all
The world? What is it you dream of, now happily,
Now sadly? Whither has the unknown call borne you?

But one moment—and the light's gone out! Habitually
And docilely you reenter the conversation that's begun.
And like a tiny light, far-off, we barely see
The indifferent gleam of your extinguished gaze.

d.

The sounds have trembled and melted
And fled to the measureless horizon;
An anxious heart's torments have been soothed,
Submerged in an objectless sorrow!

These sounds have carried far away
All visions of earthly things,
Wept, quietly petitioned,
And grown silent in mournful anxiety.

The familiar sounds rejoiced,
Returning from dark distances.
For the momentary separation's torment
How much happiness they promised!

And receiving the unexpected tidings,
The heart was apparelled in radiant dreams,
And answering the call of paradise
It grew bright with a flame of purest red.

Three Meetings*

(Moscow-London-Egypt, 1862-75-76)

Triumphing beforehand over death
And through love having overcome the chain
Of aeons, eternal beloved, I will not name you,
But my tremulous song will reach your ears.

Not believing the deceitful world,
Beneath the rough crust of matter
I have touched the incorruptible royal purple
And recognized the radiance of divinity...

Have you not thrice appeared to my real sight?
You have not been a figment of the mind,
O no! As portent, help, or as reward,
Your image has come to answer my soul's call.

1.

The first time—but how long ago that was!
Thirty-six years have passed since my soul,
Then childish, unexpectedly felt love's longing
Together with the anxiety of dark dreams.

I was nine years old, and she†...she was nine too.
"It was a day in May in Moscow," as Fet‡ wrote.
I then confessed my love. Silence. O God!
I have a rival. He will answer to me!

---

* We have consulted the translation of "Three Meetings" included in Paul M. Allen's *Vladimir Soloviev: Russian Mystic*, Blauvelt, New York, 1978, pp. 345–357. We have also consulted Judith Deutsch Kornblatt's translation, "Three Encounters," as well as her notes (MS, 1997).—TRANS.

† The "she" here is just a little girl who has nothing in common with the "eternal beloved" to whom the introduction is addressed. The episode of the "duel" has an auto-biographic character.—TRANS.

A duel! A duel! At the Ascension Feast service
A stream of passionate torments coursed through my soul.
Let us lay aside... all earthly cares: drawn out,
These words of the hymn faded gradually and stopped.

The sanctuary was open... But where were priest and deacon?
Where was the crowd of praying people? Suddenly,
The stream of passions dried up without a trace.
Azure was all around; azure was in my soul.

Suffused with a golden azure, and your hand
Holding a flower that came from other lands,
You stood there smiling a smile of radiance.
You nodded to me, and vanished in the mist.

With that the childish love grew far removed
From me, my soul grew blind to earthly things...
My German nurse kept on repeating sadly:
"Volodinka, ach, how he has stupid become!"*

2.

Years passed by. A docent and a master,
I rushed abroad for the first time... Berlin,
Then Hanover, Cologne all glimmered past,
In rapid motion hiding from my sight.

Not the world's center, Paris, not Spain,
Nor the Orient's bright multicolored splash—

‡ This is a paraphrase of Afanasy Fet's (1820–1892) verse "It was a marvelous day in May in Moscow." Fet, one of the best Russian poets of the second half of the nineteenth century, was a close friend of Solovyov's.—TRANS.

* The German nurse speaks ungrammatical Russian here, using a feminine ending as the predicate to "he." We have suggested the error through inappropriate word order in English. Volodinka is a diminutive of Vladimir.—TRANS.

[100]

Rather, the British Museum* was my dream.
Nor did this place at all deceive my hopes.

Will I ever forget you, blissful half-year?
Fleeting beauty's phantoms meant nothing to my soul,
Nor did people's lives here, passions, nature.
All my soul was possessed by you alone, beloved.

Despite people's scurrying back and forth in droves
Under the din of fire-breathing machines,
Despite massive soulless edifices all around,
I am immersed in sacred quiet. I am here alone.

Cum grano salis, to be sure: I was
Alone, but surely not a misanthrope.
For people still did find their way to me.
And whom among these people should I mention?

A pity. I do not know how to put
Their names or foreign talk into my meter.
Among them were two or three British scholars
And two or three docents† from Moscow. Still,

I was often alone in the reading room,
And, credit this or not, God is my witness
That mysterious powers led me to choose for reading
Everything possible concerning her.

Whenever some sinful whim suggested to me
To open up a book "from another opera,"

---

* Solovyov studied mystical literature at the library of the British Museum from the
end of June to the middle of October 1875.—TRANS.

† While in England Solovyov made the acquaintance of W. Ralston (1829–1889), a
writer and employee of the British Museum; and the zoologist Wallace (1822–1913). He
also made the acquaintance of two Russian docents who were law scholars: I.I. Yanzhul
(1846–1914) and M.M. Kovalevsky (1851–1916).—TRANS.

Such trouble would ensue from this
That, quite confused, I'd leave for home.

But once—it was in autumn—I said to her:
"O blossoming of divinity! I feel
Your presence here. But why have you not revealed
Yourself to my eyes since I was a child?"

Hardly had I thought these words
When all around was filled with golden azure
And before me she was shining again—
But only her face, it was her face alone.

That instant was one of happiness much prolonged.
My soul again became blind to things of earth.
And if I spoke, any "sober" ear
Would consider my speech incoherent and stupid.

3.

I said: "Your face has been revealed to me.
But I would still wish to see all of you.
You were not stingy with the child, and so
Why is it that you should refuse the youth?"

"Go then to Egypt!" sounded a voice inside me.
To Paris! And then steampower bore me southward.
Feeling did not have to fight with reason:
Reason remained quite silent—like an idiot.

To Lyons, Turin, Piacenza, and Ancona,
To Fermo, Bari, then to Brindisi.
Behold: across the shimmering deep-blue
I found myself being sped by a British steamer.

Credit and lodging were offered to me in Cairo
By Hotel Abbat—alas, no longer there!
A cozy, modest hotel, best in the world...
Russians were staying there, even some from Moscow.

A retired general entertained us there
With memories of his old Caucasus days.
It does no harm to name him—he's long dead.
And I have only good things to say about him.

He was the well-known Rostislav Faddeev,[*]
Retired soldier, good man with a pen.
Excellent at remembering names of coquettes.
Knowledgeable, too, about the local cathedrals.

Twice daily we sat together at the table d'hôte.
He was loquacious, he spoke merrily,
Was ever ready with some dubious anecdote,
And, in his limited way, philosophized.

I waited, meanwhile, for the promised meeting,
And suddenly, one night when all was still,
I heard, just like the wind's cool breath, these words:
"I am there in the desert. Go to meet me."

I had to walk. (For one is not transported
From London to the Sahara for nothing.
A marble might have rolled round my empty pocket—
For days on end I had been living on credit.)

God alone knew whither, without provisions
And without money, one fine day, I went,
Like Uncle Vlas, composed without revisions
By Nekrasov. (There, I've somehow found a rhyme.)[†]

---

[*] Rostislav Faddeev (1824–1883) was a general of the Russian army (retired 1868) and a military writer.—TRANS.

Surely, you must have have been laughing at me when I,
Attired in tall top-hat and warm overcoat in the desert,
Was taken, by sturdy bedouins, for a demon,
Provoking a shiver of fear in them and thus

Was nearly killed. When, in the Arab manner, noisily,
Sheiks of two tribes held a council to decide
My fate, then later tied my hands together
Like a slave's and without mincing words

Led me some distance off, and generously
Untied my hands—and then departed. Now
I'm laughing with you, my beloved: gods and men alike
Can laugh at troubles once they've passed.

By that time the mute night had descended
Directly to the earth. Around me I heard
Only the silence, and saw the darkness
Between the little starry flames.

Lying upon the ground, I looked and listened...
I heard the sinister wailing of a jackal,
Who was dreaming, most likely, of devouring me,
And I'd not brought even a stick to ward him off.

Yet worse than the jackal was the piercing cold...
It now was zero perhaps, and yet the day had been hot.
The stars shined mercilessly clear.
Their shining and the cold warred with my sleep.

Long I lay there in a frightened slumber, till
At last, I heard a gentle whisper: "Sleep, my poor friend."

† The device of finding a rhyme is one that is hallowed Pushkin's example. The use
of this device here is the more forgivable that the author, being not so much young as
inexperienced, is making his first try at a narrative poem. [Nikolai Nekrasov (1821–1878),
one of the most celebrated writers of his time, was known mainly for civic and political
verse.—TRANS.]

Then I fell into a deep sleep; and when I waked
The fragrance of roses wafted from earth and heaven.

And in the purple of the heavenly glow
You gazed with eyes full of an azure fire.*
And your gaze was like the first shining
Of universal and creative day.

What is, what was, and what will be were here
Embraced within that one fixed gaze... The seas
And rivers all turned blue beneath me, as did
The distant forest and the snow-capped mountain heights.

I saw it all, and all of it was one,
One image there of beauty feminine...
The immeasurable was confined within that image.
Before me, in me, you alone were there.

O radiant one! I'm not deceived by you.
I saw all of you there in the desert...
And in my soul those roses shall not fade
Wherever it is the billows of life may rush me.

A single instant! Then the vision was hidden
And into heaven's dome the solar sphere began its rise.
The desert was silent, but my soul was praying
And church bells kept on ringing in my soul.

My spirit was strong! But for two days I'd fasted
And visions of higher things began to fade.
Alas! However sensitive one's soul,
Starvation never can be a friend, they say.

Toward the Nile I followed the sun's westward path,
And in the evening I returned to Cairo.

* A paraphrase of a line from Lermontov's poem "How often when surrounded by a
motley crowd."—TRANS

[105]

Though my soul preserved the traces of your rosy smile,
Many holes had worn their way into my boots.

Viewed from the outside it was all quite stupid.
(I gave the facts but I concealed the vision.)
After he ate his soup quite wordlessly,
The general, gaze fixed at me, grandly began:

"While intelligence gives one the right to be stupid,
It's surely better not to abuse the privilege:
All told, people's obtuseness isn't quite adept
At drawing distinctions between types of madness.

And therefore, if it would offend you
If anyone considered you demented
Or merely a fool, then make no further mention
Of this inglorious adventure to anyone."

His witty utterances flowed on, but before me
The azure mist kept sending out its radiance,
And, defeated by the mysterious beauty,
The ocean of humdrum life receded far away.

****

Still slave of this vain world, this then was how
Beneath the rough crust of matter, I came to see
The incorruptible royal purple
And felt the radiance of divinity.

Overcoming death by premonition,
Through dreams having triumphed over the chain
Of aeons, eternal beloved, I will not name you,
But pardon, for your part, my feeble song!

(26–29 September 1898)

AUTHOR'S NOTE: The autumn evening and the dense woods inspired me to reproduce in comic verse the most significant thing that had ever happened in my life. For two days the memories and accords rose up irrepressibly in my consciousness. And on the third day this short autobiography, which has pleased some poets and some ladies, was ready.

The White Lily

Or a Dream on the Night of Pokrov*

A MYSTERY-JEST IN THREE ACTS

Characters of the Play

THE CHEVALIER DE MORTEMIR.† A rich but completely disillusioned landowner.

CHALDEAN. He serves in the Asiatic department, is practical.

INSTRUMENT. A retired dragoon. Has physical strength and is prepared.

SORVAL. A young man. Often does the opposite of what he says.

COUNT MNOGOBLIUDOV. Afflicted with softening of the brain tissues.

---

* Pokrov (*Pokrov Presviatoi Bogoroditsy*, or Protection of the Mother of God), celebrated on 1 October (old style) is one of the great feast days of the Russian church, and one of the primary feast days of the Mother of God. There is a belief that dreams dreamt on Pokrov always come true. — ED.

† The name Mortemir appears to be a combination of the French *mort* (death) and the Russian *mir* (the world), possibly indicating that he is "dead to this world." The name Mnogobliudov means "many dishes." Khlestakov, derived from *khlestat'* (to lash out), is the name of the protagonist of Gogol's *The Inspector General*. Chaldean can mean a member of the ancient Semitic nation, the Chaldeans; a person versed in the occult arts; or a member of a Uniate church in Iran and Iraq converted from Nestorianism in the sixteenth century. The name Sorval makes one think of the verb *sorvat'* (to tear off). A *sorvanets* is a wild, madcap fellow. — ED.

GENERAL KHLESTAKOV. He wrote all of Plato's dialogues, and was the secret cause of the head-cold that prevented Napoleon from crushing the Russian army at Borodino.

MELANCHOLY LANDOWNER. He has devoted himself to the study of transcendental physics.

SKEPTIC. He serves in the Ministry of Finances.

DON'T-SPIT-ON-THE-TABLE. An ancient sage.

GALACTEA, ALCONDA, TEREBINDA. Three ladies, agreeable in all respects.

THE SUN. A fixed star of the third magnitude.

BIRDS.

PLANTS.

WOLF.

LIONS AND TIGERS.

MOLES.

OWLS.

VOICE FROM THE FOURTH DIMENSION.

BEAR.

THE WHITE LILY.

The first act takes place in Petersburg, the second in an unknown forest, the third near southern Tibet.

ACT ONE

A winter garden in the home of the Chevalier de Mortemir. Music and the drone of conversations drift in from afar.

Scene One

Melancholy Landowner enters, tieless and wearing an unbuttoned jacket. He is accompanied by Skeptic.

MELANCHOLY LANDOWNER:

> Upon the fourth dimension
> I hourly reflect.
> In perfect enervation
> I am perishing in vain.
> Either utterly immobile do I sit
> Or else I flit about like a pale shade.
> But I could, after all, receive from my estate
> An income that's respectable!
> But, captivated without measure
> By the fourth dimension,
> I live, deprived of everything,
> In the most pathetic of states.
> And though I soon will die,
> A recipient of public assistance,
> Yet the question of the fourth dimension
> Remains unresolved.

SKEPTIC:

> O, how happy you are compared with me,
> For you have found some object for your thoughts.
> In vain have I sought something to seek with my soul.
> There is neither goal nor path before me.
> In the evening and the early morning,
> In the daytime and at full midnight,
> In heat, in frost, amid hurricanes,

I do nothing but shake my head.
I fix my gaze upon the earth
Or I stare up at the sky
Or I listen to the rustling of the trees,
Trying to divine my fate...
What road should I choose?
Whom should I love? What should I seek?
Should I go into the temple to pray to God?
Or into the woods—to kill passersby?

SCENE TWO

They are joined by Desperate Poet.[*]

DESPERATE POET:

    I am twenty years old.
    And I'm a poet—
    A poet of cosmic sorrow, sir.
    My hair has grown gray,
    A result of meditation.
    I walk about slightly hunched.
    From drinking, eating,
    Lying, sitting,
    I am prevented by
    My hemorrhoids...
    And thus the bloom of life,
    Having, under the scourge of troubles,
    Withered, fades.
    My ideal
    Was lost long ago.
    In my soul is bitter frost.
    Only in sleep's dreams
    Will there be a glimmer of her,
    Like a rainbow above storm clouds!
    But soon as I wake up
    And look about—

---

[*] Desperate Poet is not listed among the Characters at the beginning of the play. — ED.

All around me once again is loathsome:
A swarm of sorrows
And my hemorrhoids—
Truly, hemorrhoids!
I cannot live this way!
Receive me,
O death, into thy embrace!
Though I am not a saint,
There is little likelihood
That I shall land in hell.
I'm cold...
The bottom of the grave
Awaits this poet.
Nothing can save me!
Observe, world,
How a genius perishes!

[*He takes a rope out of his trousers' pocket to strangle himself, but, instead, a piece of red paper falls onto the floor.*]

MELANCHOLY LANDOWNER AND SKEPTIC:

[*Picking up the paper and triumphantly showing it to the Poet.*]

This state banknote
Will save us from ruin, O poet!

DESPERATE POET:

[*In ecstasy.*]

The horizon shines with new hope!
My dawn has risen in my trousers' pocket.
[*He takes and examines the banknote.*]
This remains from the recompense
Given to me by the bookseller...
Let's go to Palkin's... No... to Small Yaroslavets!*

[*He locks arms with Melancholy Landowner and Skeptic, and leaves together with them.*]

---

* These are Petersburg restaurants.—ED.

[113]

SCENE THREE

Galactea and Chaldean enter

GALACTEA:

You know, he's departing... It's a big secret. He asked me not to tell any-
one. I'm sad... You can't imagine how much I'm losing. *La vie s'en va.*
Nothing gives me joy any more. Nothing interests me.

[*She looks at him intently.*]

You know, you have a very handsome nose. I hadn't noticed that before.

[*She goes up to the window.*]

Behold. What a rapturous night it is. How brightly the stars shine, quite
as in Tyutchev's verses.*

CHALDEAN:

[*Looking from behind her shoulder.*]

> You are peering at the stars, my bright star...
> O, to be the sky, to hold you
> In my broad embrace and with myriads of eyes
> To admire you in your wordless radiance...

GALACTEA:

Aha! You're speaking in verse, I think? I love verse about my beauty very
much. Tell me, are you Italian?

[*Aside*]

My God, how handsome his nose is!

CHALDEAN:

No, I'm not Italian. But I can be.

GALACTEA:

I had forgotten you're Chaldean.

CHALDEAN:

---

* Fyodor Tyutchev (1803–1873) was one of the greatest Russian lyric poets of the
nineteenth century. — ED.

O, that is nothing more than a calembour of fate.

GALACTEA

Calem-bour? Wherever did you get that from? On the contrary, he's a marvelous colorist. But what is your nationality?

CHALDEAN:

That's a fearful mystery. But I'll tell you...

[*He whispers in her ear.*]

I'm a Georgian!

GALACTEA:

[*Rapturously.*]

A Georgian!!

(*She leaps about and claps.*]

He's a Georgian! He's a Georgian!

CHALDEAN:

[*Very satisfied with himself.*]

I'm a Georgian! I'm a Georgian!
And I alone know it.

GALACTEA:

[*Ecstatic*]

He's a Georgian! He's a Georgian!
And he alone knows it!

[*They take each other by the hand and hurry away.*]

SCENE FOUR

Terebinda and Instrument enter.

TEREBINDA:

Why are you not a cuirassier?

INSTRUMENT:

In twenty-four hours I will be a cuirassier.

[115]

TEREBINDA:

Do you know what my desire is now?

INSTRUMENT:

I don't know. But I will fulfill it immediately.

TEREBINDA:

I desire to be wrapped in a blanket, in nothing but a blanket. Do you understand? And I want some terribly tall and strong man, some giant or Patagonian, to carry me in his arms in a large dark garden...

INSTRUMENT:

[*Getting up.*]

I'm ready.

TEREBINDA:

Ha! Ha! Ha! Are you a Patagonian?

INSTRUMENT:

[*Wiping his face with a handkerchief.*]

A Patagonian through and through, as you see.

TEREBINDA:

What foolishness. But what's wrong with you?

INSTRUMENT:

I'm hot.

TEREBINDA:

But why?

INSTRUMENT:

> I'm hot because I love you.
> Though I know that, in the end, I shall perish,
> Yet, like a candle, I am burning.
> Like a candle, I am burning and melting, like a candle.
> But you? You're clothed in an icy garment,
> Like marble. You're deaf to my desperate prayer!
> I'm hot because you're cold!

TEREBINDA:

O yes, I'm very cold. I'm cold but curious. I would be interested in seeing
how far your flaming passion could go. *Donnez-moi le bras.*

[*They leave.*]

SCENE FIVE

Alconda enters and throws herself on a sofa.

ALCONDA:

My God, how tired I am! *Je n'en puis plus!* And that dumb bear, Sorval,
mangled my foot. In my whole life, I have never seen such an idiot.

SCENE SIX

Sorval enters.

SORVAL:

You have been seeking solitude? I too! And so, in our solitude, we are
here united.

[*He sits down next to her. There is a period of silence.*]

Will you permit me to moisten the lap of love with the tears of despair?

ALCONDA:

What's wrong with you? Sit a little farther away, please!

SORVAL:

Give me your hand!

ALCONDA:

Well, what's next?

SORVAL:

I think that if this hand were yours, I mean if it were mine, and if my
heart... No, I cannot speak any more... If you don't come to love me,
I'll...

[*He spreads his arms out wide and opens wide his mouth and eyes.*]

ALCONDA:

Love you?... Love is a fine thing, but only not here, not here...
Ah, why was a I born a maiden
Among these repellent people,
And not a feathered bird free
Amid the expanses of forests and fields.
Upon the tops of green trees,
Under the bower of shady gardens,
In garments of down and feathers,
And with fresh fruits as my food,
That is how I would wish to live and love.
That is when my soul would blossom!
How exquisitely then would I fly,
How intricately I would weave my nest!
But here, among all of you, in the midst of this furniture, in these houses
and on these streets...

SORVAL:
Why on the street?!

ALCONDA
Dieu, qu'il est bête. And then you know, I can't bear anything that runs
counter to aesthetics, anything crude. But you have, I have heard, horri-
bly crude habits. My uncle Mnogobliudov has seen you eat fish with a
knife, and he's seen you eat game—with your hands!

SCENE SEVEN

Count Mnogobliudov appears in the doorway.

COUNT MNOGOBLIUDOV
Yes, young man, I have said, and now I confirm, that you don't know
how to eat!

[*He passes through.*]

SCENE EIGHT

SORVAL:
If that's the only thing wrong, I'll stop eating fish and game. I would will-
ingly sacrifice my love at the altar of all these animals. That is, I wanted to

say just the opposite, but no matter... Alconda! As long as we are alone, I must pay tribute to my raptures!

[*He wants to embrace her.*]

ALCONDA:

(*Pushing him away*)

I think you've lost your mind.

SORVAL

As you wish, but my love demands food.

[*He grabs her by the foot, takes off her shoe, and hurriedly shoves it into his mouth. But he begins choking on her high heel and falls on the floor in convulsions.*]

ALCONDA:

Poor baby! Nobody does it that way! You always have to start with the toe of the shoe.

SCENE NINE

Count Mnogobliudov appears in the doorway.

COUNT MNOGOBLIUDOV:

I told you he doesn't know how to eat!

[*He passes through.*]

SCENE TEN

Alconda and Sorval, who is rolling on the floor in convulsions.

ALCONDA:

He could die like this! Anyone there? Hurry, hurry! *Au secours, au secours!* Some salt, some salt!

SCENE ELEVEN

From different sides of the stage enter, running, a servant with a salt-shaker on a tray, General Khlestakov, Chaldean and Galactea, Instrument and Terebinda.

[119]

GENERAL KHLESTAKOV:

Behold! Behold! Come and admire! Behold our younger generation! He can't even swallow a lady's shoe! He's choking on it. Honest to God, he's choking! What do you think of that? In the olden days, I could swallow a dozen Wellington boots, spurs and all—and nothing would happen! Except they would jangle in my stomach.

ALL:

[*Stand around Sorval and sing in chorus.*]

Ah, poor Sorval!
He's shoved a shoe down his throat
And he could die.
He has to be rubbed down
With vodka!

[*They pull the shoe out of Sorval's mouth and revive him.*]

SORVAL:

Having failed to choke myself,
I would like to depart!

ALL:

[*Politely.*]

We shall depart with pleasure
And leave you two alone.

> *All exeunt on one side, Sorval and Alconda on the other. The stage remains empty for a period of time.*

SCENE TWELVE

The Chevalier de Mortemir enters in travelling attire and carrying a suitcase. He sets it down on the floor, and stands pensive for some time, his head bowed. He then speaks.

MORTEMIR:

In profound anguish, as if bound in chains,
I stand here and stare at the ground.
Though my suitcase has long been packed,
Yet I do not depart.

[120]

[*Pause*]

If the autumn wind has pitilessly blown away
All that your soul has admired in life,
If the garden of your dreams has faded irrevocably,
If the staff of your faith has been broken…

Scene Thirteen

Galactea enters.

GALACTEA:

When, dear friend,
Will we see you again?

MORTEMIR:

[*Not hearing her*]

Yes, my flame is extinguished.
My fire has gone out!

GALACTEA:

Tell me, when?

MORTEMIR:

Only God knows!
Where I am going
There are no roads back.

GALACTEA:

What? Your love for me has
Already grown stale?

MORTEMIR:

O no! But it is as if my blood
Has frozen within me.

GALACTEA:

[*Ironically*]

O, that is because
You have loved without measure!

MORTEMIR:

What purpose have you in reproaching me?
I feel bad enough even without that.

[*After a pause*]

I have loved, even though with each one of my thoughts
I have recognized the deceit of love.
And I have tried to catch with insane thirst
The fleeting mist.
But I have barely looked into
The contemptible scroll of the passions
And have pushed aside the poisoned drink
Without drinking it to the dregs.

GALACTEA:

O my God: "barely"?!
Where did you learn to lie so?
But here is my hand—
You have not said farewell to me…

MORTEMIR:

O, do not consider me ungrateful!
I have loved you more than the others.
Like a radiant meteor,
You have flashed by in the darkness of my days.

GALACTEA:

Si c'est ainsi, I am, perhaps, still
Willing to shine in the darkness of your days.

MORTEMIR:

Merci! In my soul, withered and weary,
You have learned the knack of exciting new fires.

[*He tries to embrace her.*]

GALACTEA

[*Resisting him.*]

Tell me first why you're deserting
Your friends.

MORTEMIR:

Ah, darling. There is much you don't know
Of my fate.

[*He clasps her tightly in his arms*]

VOICE FROM THE FOURTH DIMENSION:

[*Heard only by Mortemir.*]

How sweet it is to be a monster
And how pleasant to forget
God!
But in that case our road
Is pretty
Bad!

MORTEMIR:

[*Jumping away from Galactea.*]

Excuse me, please!

GALACTEA:

[*Thinking the words are addressed to her.*]

I see you are playing the hypocrite with me,
O Mortemir!

MORTEMIR:

Ah, you would never believe how nauseated
It makes me just to look at the world!

GALACTEA:

[*Taking three flowers of unusual form from her corset and handing
them to Mortemir.*]

Our whole life is deceit, longing, and tears.
And its end is—the grave.
To remember me by, my friend, I am leaving you
Three magical roses to let
You awaken within yourself at least
The phantom of rapturous moments,
To keep your genius from being crushed

By the heavy burden you bear.

MORTEMIR:
And so, farewell!

GALACTEA
But what shall I tell
Your guests?

MORTEMIR
Tell them I've gone to the Crimea
To visit my sister there.

[*Galactea embraces him and exits.*]

SCENE FOURTEEN

*Mortemir is alone. He raises Galactea's roses to his face, and then,
slowly dropping them, he speaks.*

MORTEMIR:
Pleasure there is in the smell of roses
When a fire burns in the breast
And the whole world of magical dreams
Speaks distinctly with the soul;
When in the bluing mist the path
Of everyday existence lies before you
But the goal has been reached beforehand
And victory has anticipated the battle;
When from your heart the silvery threads stretch forth
Into the realm of reverie...
O gods eternal! Take the bitterness
Of my experience and return to me
The whole power of the first storms of spring!

———————————————

Yes, I knew you, golden years,
Dreams innocently bold,
Proud surges of freedom,
Visions of mysterious beauty,

When the distant notes of a keyboard
Or the rustling of a dress on sand
Submerged the whole soul in dreams
And excited incomprehensible longing
Or sweet trepidation.
Where are you, captivating dreams
And sorrows without cause?
The thrust of life's wave
Has borne you far away.
The turbulent surges have rushed you away,
The first roses of spring,
And where you are buried
Other flowers have bloomed
And just as quickly faded,
Or withered in an untimely way.

———————————

But let all that has come before be forgotten
And shrouded in darkness for ever!
I will make room for hope!
Perhaps I will yet succeed in finding the White Lily.
And so—forward!
Let me proceed on my mysterious quest!

[*The noise of an approaching crowd is heard.*]

Farewell all! my soul would
Find it painful to see you.
But where is my travelling cap?
Here! And my gloves are in it.

[*He leaves hurriedly.*]

ACT TWO

A picturesque meadow in an unknown forest. Sunset.

SCENE ONE

THE SUN:
Once again I am setting,
And I look about sadly:
I have not seen her today either.
O sorrow! She is nowhere to be found.
Without her the whole white world
Is no dearer to me than the nether world.

[*The Sun covers his face with clouds, and cries a fine rain.*]

BIRDS:
We sing. We sing.
Together with the sun we wait
For the golden-haired empress to appear.
But she does not hear.
Our song will not wake her
From her deep slumber.

PLANTS:
We grow and bloom.
God gives us rain to drink.
Aromas we pour forth,
Tremble, and wait for
The mistress of paradise,
She who shines with heavenly beauty,
To appear from the dwelling place of dreams
Like an empress of flowers.

WOLF:
I am a murderer and a thief.
Bloodthirsty is my gaze.

What's more, my cowardice is extreme!
Though I am quite a villain,
Yet I, too, can
No longer bear my foul life.
Tail between my legs, I lie
And look at the sky to see
If the empress will come down from there,
The empress about whom
Both the flowers and the chattering birds
Are weaving their songs.

CHORUS OF LIONS AND TIGERS:

Yyyes!
We live by violence,
Pull off the skins of those we meet,
Eat them raw,
Drink their hot blood,
But we too are waiting for
Something; secretly
We shed tears at night
And, wagging our tails,
Think of putting an end
To this kind of life...
Yyyes!

ALL:
Sun, sun! If only you would draw and lure
The empress of beauty to us
By your flaming power,
By a rainbow net of rays!
We no longer have the strength to wait for her.
Without her, all things are repulsive to us.
Lost is the luster of both day and night.
Without her, the whole world's a grave!

[*The Sun waves his hand and sets.*]

[127]

Scene Two

The Chevalier de Mortemir enters.

MORTEMIR:
She! She is everywhere! Only about her
Do all the voices of yearning nature speak.
Not I alone—but also the river, the forest, the mountains,
The trees, the beasts, the sun, and the flowers—
Call her and await her.
If she were to come, the snowy peaks
Of the cloud-piercing mountains would at once
Bow down before her; the sumptuous flowers
Would unfurl their wide carpet before her;
The lions, snow leopards, and rhinoceroses
Would gather around her,
A happy family, harmonious,
And serve her; the rapid and noisy streams
Would suddenly stop; the turbulent ocean itself
One last time would boil up again
And, after casting all of its pearls
At her feet, would grow quiet and still,
And like a mirror, transparent, motionless,
Would lie down before her so as to reflect
All the more clearly her marvelous image
In mute ecstasy. Yes, this is true!
But, my God, when?
When, when? This insignificant word
Contains despair and joy, life and death.

[*He lies down beneath a tree.*]

Scene Three

MOLES:
Holes we dig, dig, dig,
And bury food for the winter.
We do not bestow attention
Upon what our eyes do not see.

What are all these birds singing about?
What are the flowers talking about?
The beauty of some maiden-empress!
Well, that is not enough to entice us.

    OWLS:
In the ruins of castles, in ancient churches
We like to nest and luxuriate.
When all around has changed.
They alone remain the same.

We love rotted stumps. Mold is dear to us.
Rust delights us.
Only the sun's shining and bright colors
Repel us.

Graves attract us. And we even
Bring forth our offspring at graveyards.
Fallen leaves and dry moss are
The seasoning to our meals.

We believe in bliss, but just for ourselves.
For others we believe in the torments of hell!
Then we will take full delight, but now
We hold prayer services out of boredom.

But in these occupations we are perturbed by the news
Of this new empress, she
Whose coming is so insolently awaited
By all the beasts and birds of day.

SCENE FOUR

Chaldean runs in carrying a suitcase.

    CHALDEAN:
From my beautiful beloved
Have I fled into these terrifying woods.

[129]

How much unnecessary grief
Had I from her—O I who am so unfortunate—
It is impossible to say!
Finally, the time had come,
And I no longer had the strength
To bear this burden.

[*He notices Mortemir and goes up to him.*]

I will tell you as a friend:
I was about to kill my charming friend,
But as soon as the thought came into my mind,
She figured it out,
And I had to flee.

SCENE FIVE

The former two are joined by Instrument.

INSTRUMENT:
From my beautiful beloved
Have I fled into these terrifying woods, etc.

[*He notices Mortemir and Chaldean, and goes up to them.*]

I will tell you in confidence:
I had made up my mind to strangle
This beloved of mine,
But then I felt pity for her
And, grabbing my bag and stick,
I ran away as fast as I could.

SCENE SIX

Sorval runs in without any baggage, and wearing night garments.

SORVAL:
From my terrifying beloved
Have I fled into these beautiful woods, etc.

[*He notices the others and goes up to them.*]

Let me tell you in confidence
That she had already
Shot at my stomach
But the revolver misfired
And, turning over the table and candle,
I ran away as fast as I could—and here I am.

All three together
We ran for three days and three nights.
We're so hungry we could die!

CHALDEAN:
But now there's no danger.
And so, here's my counsel:
Allow me to propose to all
That you drink some vodka and have a bite to eat.

[*He takes food and drink from his suitcase, and all arrange them-selves under a tree.*]

SORVAL AND INSTRUMENT:
We willingly take this counsel,
And congratulate one another with deliverance.

[*They clink glasses.*]

CHALDEAN:
From mistresses and wives
I'm forever emancipated.
In the presence of nature
I drink to freedom!

ALL:
Hooray!

CHALDEAN:
Look: What strange figure approaches?

SORVAL:
Judging by his clothes, it must be an animal fossil.

INSTRUMENT:

But judging by his nose, it must be a monk or cobbler.

CHALDEAN:
So much the better. A new drinking mate.

SCENE SEVEN

Don't-spit-on-the-table approaches in unusual semi-Asiatic attire and with a staff.

CHALDEAN:
Listen, esteemed sir! Allow me to offer you a morsel to eat and some wine.

SORVAL:
Though your clothing shows that you were born before the invention of food and drink, join our company, I beg you. As the saying goes, the yid*
strangled himself for the sake of company.

CHALDEAN:

[*Pouring vodka*]

Or perhaps you like bordeaux?

DON'T-SPIT:
I would like both vodka and bordeaux.
Even though excess repels me,
I am ready nonetheless to eat
And drink all that I am given.

[*He sits down and drinks.*]

I did not expect to find such a meeting
In these dark woods!

CHALDEAN:

---

* This Russian saying uses the offensive word for Jew (*zhid*). It is regrettable that Solovyov chose to use this word in his play. But it should be noted that, unlike some other nineteenth century Russian writers, there was not a shred of anti-semitism in Solovyov. He always expressed great respect and admiration for Judaism, worked in behalf of Jewish civil rights, and took a deep interest in the Old Testament and Jewish mysticism. He even lectured about the Old Testament prophets to Jewish groups. — ED.

But who are you?

DON'T-SPIT:

I shall answer
Right away, but first you must do me one service.
From Kuku-Nora through Kaluga
I walked in order to find
One whose name is known to all
In Kashmir, in all of Tibet and Pamir.
I am speaking of the Chevalier de Mortemir.
Do you know him?

ALL:

There he is!

DON'T-SPIT:

[*To himself.*]

I am burning with impatience
To open my package before them.

[*He gets up and, after taking a tied-up package from his shirt, addresses Mortemir.*]

Courteous chevalier! You see before you,
Frail in body but vigorous in soul,
A servant of the science of sciences.
In my travelling cape and leaning on a staff,
I've come from far away to bring you
Unexpected but glad tidings.
Read and consider this! In the ruins
of Palmyra have I found this parchment!

[*He unties the package, removes the parchment, and hands it to Mortemir.*]

I studied it in the quiet of nights,
And accidentally made those holes with a cigarette.

MORTEMIR:

[*He reads.*]

[133]

"Abracadabra, abracadabra.
There is an elevated and mysterious meaning here
That can be revealed only by a bear
Endowed with extraordinary strength.
And the eternal-feminine element
Will not fail to play a part here:
When the azure pigment
Delivers the soul from callouses,
Then the grace of the white lily
Will everywhere pour forth its tincture
And the human race, forgetting to suffer,
Will embrace all of nature.
Peace and harmony
Will be everywhere established,
And evil and suffering will vanish.
Then you too, Mortemir,
Will find peace for your soul."
Whatever does this mean?

DON'T-SPIT:
Don't pretend!
I know everything. Asleep and awake,
You seek the White Lily,
And I am able to tell you
Where you can find her.
I know all the pathways to her,
And I'm summoning fellow-travellers.
When, ripping Palmyra apart,
I found this parchment,
It was exactly twice as long
And contained all that was necessary.
Though unfortunately—I won't attempt to hide it—
I have lost half of it.
But so often have I repeated
All the directions in my mind,
That, even at this very moment, I could
Lead you there without hesitation.
My mind is sharp and my spirit is bold!

[To the others.]

Friends! To you too I propose:
Follow me to the lost paradise.

CHALDEAN AND INSTRUMENT:
Why not? As things stand, there's else nothing to do!

SORVAL:
But what is this White Lily, esteemed sir? A woman?

DON'T-SPIT:
Something of the sort.

SORVAL:
Hm! A woman. But without a revolver?

DON'T-SPIT:
Without a revolver, without a rifle!
I can assure you!

SORVAL:
Well, then. I agree. Long live the White Lily!

DON'T-SPIT:

[Looking at the wine.]

Yes, the White Lily, yes!
And so, what should we do, sirs?

ALL:
If we're going, let's go!

DON'T-SPIT:
It would be better for us to go at dawn,
But meanwhile these bottles
Will give us strength
And keep us from catching a cold.

ALL:
That's true! That's true!
Let's wait for the sky to grow red

In the east, and meanwhile
Let us fortify ourselves a bit.

[*They eat and drink.*]

CHALDEAN:
Shouldn't we sing a song, my friends?

DON'T-SPIT:
I am always at your service.

INSTRUMENT:
Chaldean, you start singing first.
Don't clown around, just begin.

CHALDEAN:

[*Sings.*]

I have won the freedom I wanted,
The freedom that beckoned me from afar, like a treasure.
Why this unexpected longing?
Why does this freedom not bring gladness?
My heart aches and my arms fall to my sides.
All around is so dim and God-forsaken
And has been since that fateful moment
Of parting, O my cruel, my sweet friend.
Now you sing, Instrument.
Well, Instrument?

INSTRUMENT:
Give me a minute.

[*Sings.*]

We met for a reason,
And it's for a reason
My passion is like a fire!
These fiery torments are
But true guarantees
Of the power of life.
Into the fiery chasm of darkness
Eternal love

Pours its living stream,
And from the flaming dungeon
I shall once again
Retrieve for you
A feather of the Fire-bird.
The light shines from darkness.
Above the black clods of soil
The visages of your roses
Would not be able to rise
If their dark root
Were not submerged in
A womb of darkness.

[*That ends the song.*]

I cede my place to Mortemir!
Well, Mortemir? Take up the lyre!

MORTEMIR:

[*Sings.*]

Ah, far away on a Tibetan plateau
Lives my friend.
But here I pine alone in longing and sorrow.
It is dark all around.
And only at times in a mist of reveries
Do I see that
Which I could see without any trouble
A hundred years ago.
Either, having lost my strength, I shall die of longing and sorrow,
A reproach to the fates,
Or I shall find my way to that Tibetan plateau
Through Kuku-Nor.

DON'T-SPIT:
Ah, youths, youths! You are still interested in love. It's all vain. Women's
business.

CHALDEAN:
Esteemed sir! No doubt about it:

Women are trash! But it would seem that
In our present situation
We could hardly survive without them.
To elucidate my thought,
Let me sing another little song.

    (Sings.)

You honor women.
They adorn human life!
With lamb's wool
They embroider
Rugs and pillows
And knit stockings.
They cover beds
With blankets
And what's more
They are our ideals.
Without women our life
Would be devoid
Of all that is sublime and holy.
Our life would flow,
Shallow and even,
Without radiantly luminous ideas,
Without flamingly turbulent passions
And without rich impressions.
We would live alone: without children,
Without nannies, wet nurses, without laundresses, seamstresses,
And no longer would there even be husbands
With horns!

    INSTRUMENT:
Whose turn is it now? Sorval's?
Hey! Sorval, Sorval, you fool!
Sing at once, you ass.
Sorval, we're waiting for you!
Damn it! He's sound asleep.

    [*Wakes him.*]

Sing, you senseless animal!

SORVAL:

(*He sings.*)

The sun is low.
There's a blizzard outside.
My friend, turn around,
And let's depart!

[*He stops and looks questioningly.*]

ALL:
What's next?

SORVAL:
I forgot.

CHALDEAN:
You're an ass and always have been.

INSTRUMENT:
Leave him alone! Let him lie under the table!
Now, you sing us a song, Don't-spit!

DON'T-SPIT:
In a vast and dense pine forest,
Which grows on the Chukotskii peninsula—
It has many trees, many big trees—
In those wild and thick woods was I born.
I was born in the wild
And blossomed in quiet,
And did not know ruinous storms.
The years passed.
Suddenly a calamity occurred:
Our land was visited by a frost!
A terrible frost, sirs, visited us!
And this frost it was
That froze off my nose
On the Chukotskii peninsula, sirs!
And since that time

It's redder than fire—
That's what frost can do,
That's what a cruel frost can do
On the Chukotskii peninsula, sirs!

CHALDEAN:
Your nose isn't red from the cold.
Admit it: since youth you've drunk like a fish!

DON'T-SPIT:
I've drunk, I drink, and I will drink!
That is my higher calling.
They can take away my estate,
My mind, and my honor,
But what I've drunk, that,
Believe me, is mine unto my death.

MORTEMIR:
Let's stop this. It is time to go!
When that blue mountain,
With gloomy peak,
Having grown purple,
Catches on fire from the first rays of sun,
Then it will be meet for us
To step into the confines of rainbow fields.
But for the success of the undertaking,
In the battle with hostile fate,
Friends and brothers, let all of us conclude
All without the slightest exception,
An everlasting alliance among ourselves.

ALL:
Yes, yes. Touch hands!

CHALDEAN:
Though, in my opinion,
It wouldn't hurt to ask him first
If there's enough of her for all of us.

DON'T-SPIT:
Enough for all of nature, my dear man!
For all of nature, believe me!

ALL:
And so, all together now,
Let us, sirs, rush to the place
Where Lily blooms
And bliss awaits us.

DON'T-SPIT:
But allow me to ask you,
How many of us are there?

ALL:
We're five,
We're five!
Take the trouble to count:
One, two, three, four, five!
Let's count again:
One, two, three, four, five!
And so on, in infinitum.

ACT THREE

PART ONE*

A large neglected garden near southern Tibet. In the foreground is the entrance to a large cave, veiled by a purple curtain.

Scene One

Enter the Chevalier de Mortemir, Don't-spit, Chaldean, Sorval, and Instrument.

Don't-spit:

Over here, over here!
This garden, sirs,
Is the very same one
Toward which we have been heading.

All:

Yes, yes!
But what is the purpose of this cave?

Don't-spit:

There is no cave! It is only a chimera,
An illusion, a deception, a dream.
There's no reason for it to be here.
A cave can house a dragon,
Bear or lizard; but an empress—
And here I'm prepared to swear—
Could scarcely dwell in such a cave.
An empress dwells in a castle, or at the very least,
In a high tower.

Chaldean:
Where are they?

---

* Solovyov here introduces a new subdivision into the text, using a word (*stsena*) that is synonymous with the word for scene (*iavlenie*); it is translated here as part. Note also that Part One of Act Three is missing Scene Two. — ED.

[142]

DON'T-SPIT:
Don't you see those lights over there?

CHALDEAN:
Why are you lying? You can't see lights
In the brightness of day.

DON'T-SPIT:
Over here stands a tall tower, while over there
A lady is going out onto a balcony.
Surely, that must be the empress's maid,
Adorned with a feather of the Fire-bird.
She is followed by courtiers,
All wearing court-dress coats...
What do I see? They're eating pancakes!
What wonderful rich pancakes!

CHALDEAN:
He's pulling our leg, that son of the devil!

INSTRUMENT:
He treats us contemptuously!

ALL:
Beat him mercilessly!

DON'T-SPIT:
Don't be angry, my friends,
Don't judge me harshly
If I sometimes
Fool around a bit.
It's not a big deal.
As long as we have some food and drink,
Let us sit down and partake.

CHALDEAN, SORVAL, AND INSTRUMENT:
That's a great idea.
That's perfect.
We see clearly:
He's no fool.

DON'T-SPIT

[*Smugly.*]

Yes, that's clear.
I'm no fool.

MORTEMIR:

Could I eat and drink
Not knowing where she is?
There's a mystery here, I can see,
And not just one!

DON'T-SPIT:

Believe me: she has left
These regions for a reason,
But as soon as dawn's ray shines,
She will return in her chariot.

MORTEMIR:

[*Having eaten and drunk heartily, he gets up, and, pointing at the sky, he speaks.*]

Enough! I have no strength left! May my righteous anger
Strike your heart with the sting of indignation!
Have we really come here, having abandoned and contemned everything,
To drink and eat like cannibals?

ALL:

[*Hurriedly finishing their food and drink.*]

Well sir, we are ready!
What should we undertake?

MORTEMIR:

[*Somberly.*]

We must put on
The crown of thorns.

CHALDEAN:
That's certain!
But how to begin?

MORTEMIR:
I would with all my heart
Gladly tell you
If I myself
Knew how...

[*A terrible roar comes from the cave.*]

Who is sending curses
Heavenward?
There's no doubt!
There's a mystery here!
We must crawl into the cave.

DON'T-SPIT:
But first we must
Take down the curtain.
Pull it all together.
No one lag behind!

ALL:

[*They take hold of the curtain, but then Chaldean, Instrument, and Don't-spit step back, and each of them, turning aside, sings.*]

But I feel a trepidation,
Because I do not know
What awaits us,
Let me stand behind you.

[*Each of them tries to stand behind all the others. Before the curtain stand only Mortemir, deep in thought, and Sorval, looking about in perplexity.*]

DON'T-SPIT:
Dear friend, Sorval,
You should rip down the curtain!

[*He then runs even farther away.*]

SORVAL:

I obey you very willingly,
And will rip it down straightway!

> [He rips down the curtain. A large Bear comes out of the cave
> and, with a roar, stands up on his hind legs.]

DON'T-SPIT:

Ai! Ai! Ai!

> [*He grabs at his stomach, and falls dead. Sorval, Chaldean, and In-
> strument bare their swords. The Bear turns his back to them. Then,
> crossing their swords, they place Don't-spit's corpse on them and
> bear it away, singing to the tune of "How happy I am, Captain, that
> I've seen you."*]

CHALDEAN, SORVAL, AND INSTRUMENT:

He has perished, he has perished,
A sacrifice to valor.
Let our swords
Be his bier.

Wisdom with bravery
He artfully melded,
But he was suddenly slain
By this foul disease!

He has perished, he has perished,
A sacrifice to valor.
Let our swords
Be his bier.

SCENE THREE

> [*Mortemir and Bear are on stage.*]

VOICE FROM THE FOURTH DIMENSION:

The door of bliss
Then—not now—
Will be opened by the beast.
Love and believe!

[146]

MORTEMIR:
I love and believe
This beast here.

VOICE:
All right!*

PART TWO

SCENE ONE

Several weeks have passed. The scene is another place in the same garden. The cave is some distance away. In the foreground is a gravestone, near which the Chevalier de Mortemir stands in a pose of despair.

MORTEMIR

Every last nook in my soul has grown stale!
How much I loved him and how fine he was!
What grace of sprawling movements!
What genius, what wisdom
Shined from his pensive eyes! I saw in him
The last anchor of the ship of life.
He spoke in his own language,
Though without words. But with a loving soul
I could understand him easily.
And he loved me. Furry and large,
He was tender as a little child.
How he turned his beautiful head!
Alas! Those most blissful moments
Have rushed off without a trace, as in a dream.
He died... And what am I to do?
Ah, I know what! I will turn my back to nature,
Plunge a dagger into my stomach, and lie down next to him!

[*He wants to kill himself, but suddenly above the Bear's grave appears the White Lily.*]

---

* "All right" is in English in the original. — ED.

Scene Two

WHITE LILY:

From you, my darling,
I will not hide the fact
That beneath my grave
There is nothing.

MORTEMIR:

Your features are celestially fine!
But where is he, the bear of my soul?

WHITE LILY:

The Bear is alive—there is just no bear skin.
But don't grieve, my friend! This is a sacrament of nature.
I was in the bear, now the bear's in me.
As you loved him in the past, so love me now.
Invisible I was then,
But now invisible for ever
Is the beast hidden within me.

MORTEMIR:

[*Ecstatic*]

We now have bliss enough
For all eternity.
It is not for naught
That he sucked his extremity.

[*They embrace and, rising into the air, suddenly go over into the fourth dimension. White lilies and red roses grow on the former grave of the Bear.*]*

---

* In an earlier version of *The White Lily*, Mortemir and the White Lily die instantly of "an excess of bliss" when they "are united by the ties of love." Villagers find them and bury them. Red roses grow on Mortemir's grave and white lilies grow on White Lily's grave.— ED.

[148]

Scene Three

Enter Galactea, Terebinda, and Alconda

GALACTEA, TEREBINDA, AND ALCONDA:
We are tired, we are tired.
We have wandered, we've been wayward,
Lost our way, that is to say.
We awaited the unexpected,
Sought the impossible—
All for naught.

GALACTEA:
These lilies and roses
Carry us into the realm of dreams—
Should we not go to sleep?

ALCONDA:
I have not slept for two weeks.
Indeed, let us rest.

TEREBINDA:
From sorrow and care
Let's seek shelter in this grotto.

GALACTEA:
Yes, each one tying up a bouquet,
We shall enter this cave.

[*They fashion their bouquets and go into the cave.*]

Scene Four

Enter Chaldean, Instrument, and Sorval

CHALDEAN:
Look under those bushes. Look under those bushes, I tell you. What idiots!

SORVAL:
Why look? I've gotten into a heap of trouble even without looking.

[149]

INSTRUMENT:

It was washed away by rain, or blown away by wind.

SORVAL

There's something white over there.

[*He picks up a piece of paper, and throws it.*]

CHALDEAN

Yes, it's a piece of paper,
But not the one we're looking for.
Ah, you simpleton!

SORVAL:

I found it!

(*He picks up the parchment of the wise man, Don't-Spit-on-the-Table.*)

It's intact. Look.

CHALDEAN:

[*He takes it and reads.*]

"Abracadabra, abracadabra.
There is an elevated and mysterious meaning here
That can be revealed only by a bear
Endowed with extraordinary strength."
You see: a bear. Everything went as it should have. We were foolish to be
scared, and that old clown more than anyone. Mortemir's no fool: He
stayed with the bear; and now he's certainly got the White Lily, but we
have to keep skulking around here as if we were possessed.

INSTRUMENT:

We must find them.

SORVAL:

But where should we look?

INSTRUMENT:

It's obvious where. There's that very same cave.

CHALDEAN:

Sorval, my soul, run over there. Do me a great favor. Look in the cave.

SORVAL:
With great pleasure.

[*He disappears into the cave, and after a few minutes cries out.*]

Hey, hey, Chaldean!
Come quick!
Hey, Instrument,
Seize the moment!

CHALDEAN:
Whom did you find there?

SCENE FIVE

Sorval leaves the cave. He's followed by Alconda, Galactea, and Terebinda.

SORVAL:
A white lily. Look:
Not one, but three.

CHALDEAN AND INSTRUMENT:
Familiar features but with a new beauty.

CHALDEAN:

[*Pointing to Galactea*]

I am captivated by this one.

INSTRUMENT:

[*Pointing to Terebinda*]

And I by that one.

ALCONDA, GALACTEA, AND TEREBINDA:

[*Each handing her bouquet to her respective partner.*]

Dear friend, did you recognize me?
Though you sought another here,
You must submit to your fate.

[151]

CHALDEAN, INSTRUMENT, AND SORVAL

[*Each to his lady.*]

I do not regret it.
For I recognize
The White Lily in you.

[*Each pair embraces, and all coming together, they sing.*]

The White Lily with a rose,*
With a red rose, we marry.
We find eternal truth
With the heart's prophetic dream.
Say the prophetic word!

---

* This final poem is almost identical with Solovyov's poem "*Song of the Ophites*" (1876). In explicating "The Song of the Ophites," Paul M. Allen (in *Vladimir Soloviev: Russian Mystic*, Blauvelt, New York, 1978, 122–127) interprets the White Lily as symbolizing the "bearer of heavenly *wisdom* from the world of the stars to the earth" (ibid., 124). On the other hand, Allen sees the rose as representing "the forces of the *heart* which grow up in earthly men, working in perfect balance between what is above and what is below" (ibid.). It is clear that, for Solovyov, the roses stand for Mortemir, while the white lilies, of course, stand for the White Lily, or Sophia, the "bearer of heavenly wisdom." Allen comments that, "in his *Song of the Ophites* [and thus in the concluding poem of *The White Lily*—ED.] Soloviev makes use of other images as well, for example, the pearls— bringing to mind 'the pearl of great price'—which are cast into the cup, the chalice, in which the deed of a transformation, a divine Alchemy, takes place. The dove figures the Holy Spirit, which in the 'coils of the Serpent', the embrace of Christ, is at peace" (ibid., 125). The Ophites, an early Gnostic sect, "taught that the Serpent was sent as a blessing to Adam and Eve by the Sophia, but brought about their Fall and Expulsion instead. In the figure of the Christ himself the Ophites saw the Serpent returned to earth to bless humanity" (ibid., 123). Allen further notes that "the working of the Rosicrucian divine Alchemy, the marriage of the lily and the rose, the uniting of the forces of head and heart, of necessity and freedom within the human being, is pictured in these verses. The working of the Promethean fire, cutting away the fetters of the past, the chain of ancient necessity, which comes about as human beings take the first steps in the direction of true freedom, cannot frighten the heart which had found its relationship with the Christ-imbued forces of Divine wisdom, of the Sophia. The last verse pictures the mystical union; inasmuch as this brings new possibilities to birth, it creates a 'violent tempest', reminiscent of the tempest described in the opening scene of *The Chemical Wedding of Christian Rosenkreutz*. However, under the guidance of Divine Wisdom, secure and certain of the working of a divine purpose acting in human destiny, the human being finds 'rest' and calm" (ibid., 126–127).—ED.

Quickly cast your pearl into the cup!
Bind our dove
With new coils of the ancient serpent.
The free heart does not ache.
Should she fear the Promethean fire?
The pure dove feels free
In the flaming coils of the mighty serpent.
Sing of violent tempests:
In violent tempests we find peace.
The White Lily with a rose,
With a red rose, we marry.

CURTAIN

1878–1880

Appendix

THE POETRY OF VLADIMIR SOLOVYOV

By Sergius Bulgakov*

IT IS NOW IMPOSSIBLE TO DENY that Solovyov's poetry occupies an important place in Russian literature: its enchanting freshness irresistibly draws the reader, and it is a consolation to immerse one's soul from time to time in this noble wellspring. This poetry has clearly had an enormous influence on such contemporary poets as Alexander Blok, Andrey Belyi, and Vyacheslav Ivanov;† and a number of younger poets have, in a certain sense, come out of Vladimir Solovyov, whose poetic influence has become fused with that of Novalis, Goethe, and Tyutchev. In essence it is necessary to recognize that Solovyov's poetic influence is more imperceptible and subtle, but nonetheless more profound and radical, than his purely philosophical influence. Certainly, one can find numerous contemporary representatives of religio-philosophical thought in Russia who revere Solovyov as the one who first opened their eyes to religious truth, was their "guide to Christ," as it were. But, in and of

* This essay, a review of the sixth edition of the Collected Poems of Vladimir Solovyov (1915), first appeared in the journal *Russkaia Mysl'* (Russian Thought), 1915, II:5, and was later reprinted in a collection of Bulgakov's essays: *Tikhie dumy* (Quiet Meditations), 2nd edition, YMCA-Press, Paris, 1976, pp. 71–76. The prominent theologian Bulgakov is considered to be one of Solovyov's philosophical heirs, especially in the development of the doctrine of Sophia. This essay is translated here for the first time. It has been very slightly abridged for the present edition.—ED

† Blok, Belyi, and Ivanov were leading poets of the Symbolist school that dominated Russian poetry at the beginning of the 20th century. Blok and Belyi were instrumental in transmitting the idea of Sophia to the next generation of philosophers after Solovyov (most notably, Bulgakov himself and Pavel Florensky).—ED

itself, Solovyov's philosophy is gradually losing its power and even its attraction for those for whom it was once a central experience.[*]

Solovyov's poetry, by contrast, retains its fine noble freshness; and in moments of the soul's inspired quietude, the book of his poems opens as if by itself. Thus, it is becoming more and more evident that, in Solovyov's multistoried, intricate, and complex work, only the poetry is absolutely authentic, so that his philosophy can and must be checked against the poetry. That which cannot be found in the poetry must therefore be considered artificial, scholastic, or accidental in the philosophy. The poetry has no equivalent for Solovyov's deductions, schemata, and categories, borrowed to a significant extent from the Germans; it has no prejudiced and somewhat opportunistic polemic with the Slavophiles; it has no multistoried and rationalistic "justification of the good."[†] On the other hand, the poetry contains everything that we find so captivating and vital in Solovyov: profound insights into the Old Testament and New Testament religion, ardent veneration of the Most Pure Virgin, adoration of "Mistress earth," the mysticism of love, a living link with those who have passed away. An inner fairness with regard to Solovyov would perhaps require us to expound his world-view precisely on the basis of his poems, while considering his prose to be a philosophical commentary to them, and not vice versa, as is done today. It is not by chance that Solovyov was so stingy when it came to writing poems, whereas he was so fluent when it came to writing articles on various themes. Perhaps, the criticism of our time will indeed carry out such a reassessment, preserving Solovyov for future generations primarily as a philosophical poet and only secondarily as a poeticizing philosopher.

Solovyov's profound personal religiosity and his personal mysticism are indissolubly linked with his poetry. It is now clear that Solovyov the mystic, with his rich and original mystical experience, is more significant, original, and interesting than Solovyov the philosopher. In fact,

---

[*] Bulgakov was clearly writing at a time (1915) when the influence of Solovyov's philosophy was waning. *Pace* Bulgakov, one must nevertheless say that Solovyov's philosophy continued to be central for many 20th century Russian philosophers, both in exile (e.g., S.L. Frank) and in the Soviet Union (e.g., A.F. Losev).—ED

[†] See Solovyov's work, *Justification of the Good: An Essay in Moral Philosophy* (1892–1984), translated by Natalie Duddington, London, 1918. New edition, Eerdman's, 2005. Edited by Boris Jakim.—ED

what would the author of *A Critique of Abstract Principles* be for us without his personal mysticism of the Eternal Feminine, without his mysterious relationship with "Sophia," a relationship that, philosophically, is so mutely and indistinctly hinted at in *Lectures on Divine Humanity* or in *La Russie et l'Eglise Universelle*,* but that is so captivatingly and vitally described in the poems? It appears that Solovyov's archive may contain many as yet unexamined materials that would shed light on his mysticism. In any case, the most striking and enigmatic feature of his poetry and of his mysticism is the concreteness of his relationship with the "Eternal Feminine," or "Sophia," of his mystical encounter with her.

Of significance, moreover, are not only the main encounters that are described in "Three Meetings" but also the more fleeting encounters, not dated precisely, that have left only a fading reflection in his poetry. Solovyov's sophianic inspiration was awakened not only by external romantic episodes of his life (when, to cite Novalis, the Divine Sophia was revealed to him through the little Sophie) but, evidently, also without any such occasion. In this sense, his sophianically erotic poetry consists, as it were, of letters without addressee, while being marked by a total concreteness of feeling. In this respect, Solovyov's poetry is unique of its kind. Read, for instance, the marvelous poem that begins with the lines:

> The instant that you doze in daytime or wake up
> At night someone is there... There are two of us.
> (see poem no. 120 in present volume)

The poems of the "sophianic" cycle sometimes have not only a poetic but even an incantatory, invocatory character. This impression is indirectly confirmed by the fact that, in 1874, when Solovyov experienced his first surge of sophianic creativity (the second was in the last years of his life), he recorded in his album the following invocatory "Prayer of the Revelation of the Great Mystery":

---

* Solovyov's *A Critique of Abstract Principles* (1880) is perhaps Solovyov's greatest work of theoretical philosophy. *Lectures on Divine Humanity* (1877–1881; Lindisfarne Books edition: 1995, revised by Boris Jakim) is perhaps his greatest work of theology. Solovyov's French work *La Russie et l'Eglise Universelle* (1888; Eng. translation by H. Rees, London, 1948) is an attempt to sketch out directions toward a reunification of the churches. —ED

In the name of the Father and of the Son and of the Holy Spirit.

An-Soph, Jah, Soph-Jah.

By the ineffable, terrible, and all-powerful name I invoke gods, demons, human beings, and all living creatures. Gather into one the rays of your power, block the source of your desires, and be participants in my prayer: that we may capture the pure dove of Sion and acquire the priceless pearl of Ophir, that the roses may unite with the lilies in the valley of Sharon. O most holy Divine Sophia, essential image of beauty and sweetness of the supraexistent God, radiant body of eternity, soul of worlds and the one empress of all souls, I implore you by the profundity of your inexpressible and gracious first son, the beloved Jesus Christ: descend into the prison of the soul, fill our darkness with your radiance, melt away the fetters that bind our spirit with the fire of your love, grant us light and freedom, appear to us in visible and substantial form, incarnate yourself in us and in the world, restoring the fullness of the ages, so that the deep may be confined and that God may be all in all.

It is true that, in and of itself, this "prayer" does not at all speak of a corresponding experience,* but it does characterize a tendency of thought and interest.

With his sophianically erotic poems, with his mystical calls and invocations, Solovyov, it would seem, transmitted a certain energy; and it may be that his calls were heard by certain sophianically gifted individuals. But were they actually heard by anyone? Who knows. Nevertheless, one fact of this kind has recently become known: Anna Schmidt in Nizhnii Novgorod heard Solovyov's call and took it as meant for her.† She said: it is about me. I am that alter ego of Solovyov that he has been awaiting and seeking. Even if one considers this mystical encounter a

---

* In a footnote, Bulgakov's expresses the opinion that this prayer was not written by Solovyov himself but is a translation of an ancient Gnostic text. — ED

† Anna Schmidt (1851–1905) was a writer for a newspaper in Nizhnii Novgorod who considered Vladimir Solovyov to be one of the incarnations of Christ and herself to be the personal incarnation of Sophia. She wrote a mystical work called *The Third Testament*, which Bulgakov considered profound (Bulgakov and Pavel Florensky were instrumental in publishing her writings). — ED

product of mystical fantasy and misunderstanding, it represents something highly interesting and not at all accidental in Solovyov's biography. It indirectly confirms the mystical realism of his sophianically erotic poetry.

In the last period of Solovyov's life, just before his death, the mystical atmosphere around him became charged once again. It was at this time that he wrote the poems "Three Meetings," "*Das ewig Weibliche*," and "*Les revenants.*" And suddenly the stretched string broke. Some sort of mysterious, purifying detachment took place: an emancipation of the soul from spells, a catharsis. And, in the final and supreme inspiration of Solovyov's muse, there sounded the pre-death song of a wounded bird. A mysterious and miraculous regeneration of the word takes place: the word appears to come from another world. Magic and invocatory spells cease. This is the song of Lermontov's "Angel,"* with which the Angel accompanies the soul into the world and calls it out of the world. The soul is once again surrounded by angelic flowers, by white bellflowers, and the heart hears their heavenly ringing:

On fierce, on broiling
Summer days
They are the same:
Shapely and white.

Let the phantoms of spring
Be burned.
Here you are, unearthly,
Truthful dreams.

Evil once experienced
Sinks down into the blood.
The sun of love,
Washed-pure, rises up.

* Lermontov's "Angel" (1831) is one of the greatest poems in the Russian language. — ED

There are bold plans
Within the heart that's sick—
White angels
Have risen all around.

Shapely and airy,
They are just the same—
On heavy, suffocating
Days, fierce days.
(see poem no. 128 in the present volume)

The fourth stanza has the variant:

There are bold plans
That grow firm in the heart.
White angels
Whisper: *come.*

Come! Thus, the poet heard the quiet approach of the white angel of
death, liberator of the poet from the fierce, suffocating July days of life.